PROACTIVE DISCIPLINE

A Parent's Guide

Second Edition

Katie Ely

ISBN-13: 978-1537498669
ISBN-10: 1537498665

DEDICATION

To my sons, Hunter and Skyler. If you hadn't grown up to be such incredible young men, I would never have had the confidence to write this book.

Contents

INTRODUCTION

Have you ever wondered how some teachers can have an entire class of well-behaved children? These are the teachers whose students walk down the hall quietly, sit still, and listen in class. How do these teachers do it?

As a teacher, I'd like to share with you some tricks of the trade on how to have well-behaved children. In my sixteen years of teaching, I've made plenty of mistakes. But from these mistakes I've learned a lot. I've attended numerous workshops, sought out the advice of exceptional teachers, and read over 40 books on discipline. With each passing year, I learned new tricks and continued old favorites of how to have well-behaved children.

One of the most important lessons that I've learned is that good discipline is proactive and not reactive. In other words, if you spend time training your children in correct behavior, you won't have to constantly deal with bad behavior.

I finally figured this out after my third year of teaching. As a beginning teacher, I would just go through the day and handle behavioral problems as they came up. The problem was they came up all day long! I would waste so much time each day dealing with misbehavior. Then I discovered the secret of training.

I learned that if I would spend time at the beginning of the school year training my students the proper way to act, I could prevent the vast majority of disciplinary problems. I called these times of instruction "Training Sessions."

During these Training Sessions, I would instruct my students exactly what they should and should not do. I was very specific. I also told them the exact consequence they would receive for breaking the rules. Then we practiced and rehearsed the correct behavior so many times it just became ingrained in their heads.

Every year, I spent the first two weeks training my students the proper way to behave in school. I trained my students how to line up, walk down the hall, and behave in the bathroom. I trained them how I expected them to sharpen their pencils, pass out papers, and clean up at the end of the day. I trained them for every aspect of the school day. By the end of the first two weeks, I had an incredibly well-behaved, well-managed classroom. My students had practiced the correct behavior so many times, it had just become habit. After the initial Training Session, all I had to do was to quickly review the rules before each activity.

While spending two weeks training my students may seem excessive, it actually saved time. Instead of wasting several minutes each day dealing with disciplinary problems, my students were well behaved and ready to learn.

After nine years of teaching, I had my own children. I realized then that the same basic discipline techniques I used at school would transfer into parenting. At home, I trained my boys what the correct behavior was for bedtime, clean-up time, shopping, mealtime, and general obedience. With my own children, however, I added another component to training. I trained not only their behavior, but I trained their hearts as well. I discovered if you train children's hearts, training their behavior is a whole lot easier!

I'm aware that most child-rearing books are written by pediatricians or child psychologists. But who would know better what really works with children than a teacher who has to be with them 7 hours a day, 180 days a year? My approach isn't a theory. This is proven advice that really works.

All the things I'm about to share I actually did with my sons. My boys are grown now and in my humble opinion, they've turned out awesome. They are both hardworking, responsible, well-mannered young men—and they love their mom!

I've done my best to make this an easy read for busy parents and to pack it with practical information. So don't wait until bad behavior happens. Read on to find out how you can be proactive, and train your children the correct way to behave in the first place.

1
THE FOUNDATION OF
EFFECTIVE DISCIPLINE: LOVE

As a teacher, I considered myself to be fairly strict. I had clear rules that I consistently enforced. I didn't allow my students to be disruptive or disrespectful. If I told them to do something, I expected them to obey. However, I wasn't known for my strictness. Instead, I believe I was characterized by my love for my students. I had them convinced that I thought they were incredibly smart, sweet, and wonderful. I smiled a lot, gave lots of hugs, and got excited to see them each day. I looked for what they were doing right and praised them for it. I tried to create a fun, positive atmosphere where my students felt cherished, safe, and comfortable. I believe all of my students knew that they were dearly loved!

Before I get into the specifics of discipline, I need to lay the groundwork. The foundation of good discipline is love. Without a loving relationship with your children, discipline will be ineffective, especially in the teen years. So if you don't intend to be heavy in love, this book is not for you. To strictly enforce rules without the undercurrent of love is not good discipline. But if you're feeling all tender and warm, keep reading. This chapter will teach you how you can lay the foundation of good discipline—love.

The Four Parenting Styles

It is generally agreed that there are four broad categories of parenting styles:

1. The Permissive Parent is high in love but low in discipline.
2. The Neglectful or Uninvolved Parent is low in both love and discipline.
3. The Dictator or Authoritarian Parent is high in discipline but low in love.
4. The Authoritative Parent is high in both love and discipline.

Studies have shown that the most effective parenting style is the authoritative parent. It's a combination of discipline and love. The authoritative parent has clear rules that are consistently enforced but in a loving manner. These parents are definitely the boss; however, their children are loved and respected. Therefore, before discipline and consequences ever take place, there must be a solid foundation of love.

Building a Loving Relationship

The most obvious way to build a loving relationship is to tell your children that you love them every single day. I'm reminded of the story of the wife who complained to her husband because he never said he loved her anymore. He replied, "I said it 40 years ago, and if it ever changes, I'll let you know." Don't assume that your children know that you love them. Children need to hear that they're loved every day. Not a day went by when my mother didn't tell me that she loved me, and that I was her greatest joy. Almost every time I got in a car she would tell the driver, "Be careful. You've got my greatest treasure in that car."

When children know that they are deeply loved, they won't resent your discipline. They may not like it, but they'll know that you have their best interest at heart. There's also another advantage. When children know that you love and admire them that much, they won't want to disappoint you. My mother once asked my brother why he didn't drink and take drugs in high school like some of the other kids. Without hesitation he replied, "Because I loved you so much, I couldn't bear to disappoint you."

Fathers especially need to make an effort to tell their children they love them. I once heard a pastor say that he had counseled scores of men who confided that their fathers had never said they loved them. Even in their adult years, it was still a painful memory.

4

In addition to telling your children you love them, write them love notes. These notes can be long or short, but tell your kids how very much you love them. Put the notes in unexpected places like their coat pockets, lunches, or under their pillow.

Children also need lots of hugs and affection. One long-term study showed that being raised with an abundance of hugs, kisses, and cuddling went further toward producing happy adults than being raised with any other advantage. Affection even helped negate poverty, broken homes, and stress.

So start the day on a positive note and cuddle with your kids when you wake them up. Give them hugs and kisses throughout the day. And always end the day with lots of affection.

When my twin boys, Hunter and Skyler, were little, I always made them give me a hug and kiss before bed. When they were in high school, I carried on that tradition. When they would come home from wherever they had been, they had to come into our bedroom, tell us they were home, and give me a hug and a kiss. Why? So I could smell their breath, that's why! I always smelled for traces of alcohol or smoke, and they knew it. It wasn't that I didn't trust my teenagers, but my motto in the teen years was to trust but verify. Since my boys knew that I was going to indirectly smell their breath, it was a mighty deterrent! (Do you see how versatile affection can be in the teen years? Giving your teen a hug and kiss before bed—especially on weekends— is a great idea!)

It's also important to make your home a refuge of unconditional love and acceptance. Let your kids know that their behavior has nothing to do with how much you love them. That's why it's so important to express your love—even when they misbehave.

Having a place of refuge also means that you listen to your children. Researchers have found that today's children often feel neglected because their parents are so involved with their cell phones or other technology that they're too busy to listen to them. So try to give your children your full attention for at least 15 minutes a day. Turn off your phone and other distractions, look them in the eye, and really listen to them. Ask them about their day. What was the best part of their day? What was the worst? Get your children into the habit of telling you about their day so hopefully they'll continue throughout their teen years.

To children, love is spelled T.I.M.E. So spend time with your kids.

While you shouldn't be your children's sole source of entertainment, play with your kids when you can. Build with construction toys, have a tea party, play ball outside, but have fun.

I know some families who schedule a Family Game Night once a week. They either play board games, charades, cards, or some other favorite. It's a great chance to strengthen the family relationship.

The goal is to build a strong, loving relationship with your kids so that when you do have to discipline them, they know you're doing it because you want the best for them.

One great idea to connect with your kids is to have a date night with them. Once a month or so, take each child out individually for a meal and/or a fun activity. Go bowling, play miniature golf, eat at a fancy tea room, or go fly a kite. And it doesn't have to be expensive. A simple picnic at the local park will have the same effect. The point is to spend quality time alone with each child and make him or her feel special.

I love the story about Charles Adams, who was the grandson of President John Adams. It seems that both Charles and his son Henry wrote in a diary every day. Years later, the two diaries were compared. When Henry was eight years old, he wrote: "Went fishing with my father today, the most glorious day of my life." In fact, the day was so glorious, Henry continued to talk and write about that particular day for the next thirty years.

However, when they looked at his father's diary entry for that same day, Charles wrote: "Went fishing with my son, a day wasted." Never underestimate the impact of time spent with your children.

Another great way to bond with your kids is to go on family vacations. And even if you can't afford a big vacation, take your kids on mini-vacations. Day trips to a state park, lake, or the zoo create memorable family experiences.

Having a network of extended family or family friends is another great way to make your children feel loved and secure. Spending time with grandparents, aunts, uncles, and cousins is good for kids. You can never have too many people who love your children. However, if your relatives live too far away, or if they are not the kind of influence you want for your children, find friends who will help love your kids and validate your morals.

I didn't live close to my family when my boys were growing up. However, my boys got very involved in our church's youth group, and my husband and I became friends with many of the youths' parents.

While the teenagers were in youth group, we parents met in our own small group. Both the parents and the youths became very close, and we became like an extended family.

I remember one particular fall day, we all met in the park for hot dogs. As the teenagers sat at the picnic tables, one of my friends gave them a sex boot camp talk. She talked about pornography, dating, sex, etc. All of us parents were standing united behind her nodding in agreement. It was amazing. I had said the exact same thing to my sons, but when I said it, I could see their eyes glaze over. But when all of their friends' parents were agreeing to the same things, it really made an impact. My boys knew as teenagers they had a large group of parents watching them.

So if you're not near an extended family, I encourage you to get involved with other like-minded parents and form a support group. Parents of teenagers need all the support they can get!

The 10-to-1 Rule

Our goal as parents should be to raise our children in a loving, positive environment. There's a great concept I've heard of called the 10-to-1 Rule. With the 10-to-1 Rule, you are to be positive ten times for every one time you are critical. This will help you gauge whether you're being too negative or not. Because your day should be characterized with love, laughter, and fun. Yes, you will have to stop and discipline when your children act inappropriately. However, you should be far more positive than negative.

Evaluate how you talk to your children. Are you more positive than negative? Do you make it evident that you love and cherish them? Do you build your children up or cut them down? Be aware of how you speak to your kids. If you hear yourself constantly criticizing, stop and try again. Train yourself to be positive with your children.

Try saying statements such as:

- I'm so proud of you!
- I'm so blessed to have you as my daughter.
- You're going to grow up to be such an amazing person.
- Your teacher is just going to love you.
- You are so kind to other people.

- You're the best son any mother could ever have!

Ever since my boys have been little, my husband and I have tried to speak words of success over their lives. In fact, that's one way I used to encourage good table manners. I would say, "Now listen, when you grow up to be the president of the company, and you're having a power lunch with a group of millionaires, you've got to have impeccable table manners. So get your elbows off the table!" Or when they would use incorrect grammar, like "Me and Matt..." I would say, "Listen when you're the head of the company, and you're in charge at all the meetings, you have to be able to speak intelligently." So I was correcting them, but at the same time telling them my expectations were great.

Catch Them Being Good

One great way to foster a positive environment and encourage good behavior, is to focus on what your children are doing right, and draw attention to that. Teachers call it 'Catch Them Being Good.' Basically, it just means to be on the lookout for when children are behaving correctly and then praise them for it.

Children crave attention, and they'll get it one way or another. If they can't get positive attention, they'll seek negative. So give them good attention and praise them when they're being good. This encourages children to get the right kind of attention.

So when your children are eating politely, make it a point to call attention to their wonderful table manners. Or, if they were quiet while you talked on the phone, tell them how much you appreciated them being quiet. Look for the good things your children do, and you'll find there's even more to come.

One note of caution: Don't over praise just to make your children feel good. Sincere, meaningful praise of a job well done is much better than lavish praise about any old thing. If all you do all day is tell your children they're the most wonderful things to ever walk this planet, your praise will become meaningless. And you might very well create spoiled brats. Tell your children when they're being good, but only when they truly deserve it.

Self-fulfilling Prophesy

"You reap what you sow" is especially true for parenting. Whatever you put into your children's mind is what is going to come out. If your children hear that they are smart, sweet, and well mannered, they're probably going to act smart, sweet, and well mannered. However, if children hear that they are stupid, mean, and rotten, they're probably going to act stupid, mean, and rotten. The words adults say about children go straight to their hearts and help determine their self-concept. And children will behave how they see themselves.

I remember once at the beginning of the school year, a mother brought her daughter in early so she could meet her new teacher. As the mother introduced her daughter to me, she said, "I'm sure you won't have any trouble with Lisa. She is so good. She always does what you tell her to." Sure enough, I never had any trouble with Lisa. She was exactly as her mother described her.

On the other hand, motivational speaker Zig Ziglar tells the story of a prisoner who overheard someone say, "I'm so glad I didn't disappoint my father." The prisoner replied, "I didn't disappoint my dad either. I'm exactly where he said I was going to be."

So be careful never to call children a derogatory name—even if you're kidding. Calling children stupid or chubby or a big baby, even in jest, can be taken to heart by children. Once children begin to think that they're bad or stupid or ugly or fat, it's hard to get rid of that self-image.

The Importance of Family Meals

Finally, one of the best ways to strengthen your family relationships is to have family meals. Research shows that not only are family dinners healthier, but children who have frequent meals with their families do better in school. And, they're less likely to engage in risky behavior such as drug and alcohol abuse, suicide attempts, violent acts, and sexual activity.

The most likely reason that research shows that children excel when they eat regular family meals is that eating together strengthens family relationships. The dinner hour provides a time when the entire family connects and participates in conversation. Children learn how to listen, interact, and expand their vocabulary. It's a time when family can find out what's going on in the lives of the other members. It's a time when you can find out if your children are experiencing any problems. It's a time when you can learn about your children's friends. It's also a great time to invite their new friends over to find out if they are appropriate for your children. Family meals are just a great opportunity for parents to subtly reinforce their values, boundaries, and expectations.

When my twins Hunter and Skyler were in high school, we spent a lot of time around the dinner table discussing their futures. We talked about the many career choices they had and which careers would realistically support a family. We discussed what steps they needed to take to prepare for college like grades, job experience, leadership roles, community service, etc. My husband even invited some of his successful friends to dinner to discuss different career options with my boys. One petroleum engineer told my son that his company wouldn't even interview applicants who had less than a 3.25 GPA. Another friend told my boys that they start with the applicants with the highest GPAs and consider these candidates first. (We frequently reminded our sons about both these points during their college years.) These dinner time conversations got my sons motivated and excited about their futures.

Now if you're thinking there is no way you have time to have family meals, remember, pizza and takeout count as a family meal. The point is just to spend some quality time together as a family.

Here are some ideas to make your family dinners a success:

- Turn off the TV and all distractions during dinner. Make it a family rule that all cell phones and other technology (including parents') are left in the bedroom.
- Ask each family member about his or her day. What was their favorite part of the day? What was the worst? Anything funny or exciting happen that day?
- Let each family member talk. Model being a good listener and train your children to do the same. Teach your children not to interrupt.
- Keep the conversations positive. Family meals are not a time to fight or bicker or bring up upsetting issues.
- Discuss current events if the children are older. Let your views be known, and let your kids express their opinions too.
- Aim to have family dinners at least three to five times a week.
- Cook as a family. Let everyone help in the preparation of the

meal. Did you know it's not uncommon for a 5-year-old in an Amish family to know how to cook? Unless your kids are toddlers, there's something they can do to help. Not only will this teach them to cook but will help them develop the character traits of helpfulness, unselfishness, and a work ethic.

- Keep it simple. Use the crockpot for easy meals that are ready when you get home.
- Have the entire family help clean up. We want to teach our children that the world does not revolve around them and that everyone has to do their part. When you make your children help clean up after a meal, you're developing their work ethic and teaching them that helping is the kind thing to do. Plus, working together as a family will strengthen the family bond.

2
THE SECRET TO HAVING
A WELL-BEHAVED CHILD: TRAINING

When most people think about discipline, they usually think about what to do *after* their child disobeys. Should they use time-out, loss of privilege, early bedtime, or what? But good discipline isn't about punishment. Truly good discipline focuses on training the right behavior in the first place before your child disobeys. In fact, the root word of discipline is disciple, which means to train.

The secret to having well-behaved children is to train them exactly how you expect them to act in every situation. They need to know exactly what they should and should not do. And they need to know the exact consequence they will receive for not following the rules.

With training you're being proactive, not reactive. You don't wait until the bad behavior happens. You train your children the correct way to behave before any misbehavior takes place.

I once heard a Green Beret say he had to train for every conceivable circumstance. He would practice over and over exactly what he was supposed to do until it became second nature.

Parents can apply this same principle of training at home. You can train your children how you expect them to act in every situation: bedtime, clean-up time, shopping, mealtime, and general obedience. You do it with Training Sessions.

These Training Sessions are just a time when you instruct, demonstrate, and have your children practice the correct behavior. You also clearly state the consequence for wrong behavior.

While it's ideal to train before the bad behavior begins, you can also train your children to undo their bad habits.

Some critics of training argue that demanding things be done in a certain way restricts children's individual freedom and stifles creativity. But without a solid foundation of right behavior and self-control, children are not going to be free to accomplish what they really want to do. Charles de Gaulle said, "Only the disciplined are free." Think about it. Who is freer? Someone obeying traffic lights or someone who is not obeying traffic lights? How free do you want your children to be? Free to break household rules? Free to be on drugs? Free to get pregnant?

Good behavior doesn't come naturally to children. It must be taught—and preferably taught before a problem arises.

How to Train Your Child with Training Sessions

The first rule of a Training Session is to schedule it at a neutral time, not when the poor behavior is taking place. Plan the Training Session when you have plenty of time, and both you and your children are well rested and in a good mood. So if you're training for bedtime, don't do it at night when everyone is tired and cranky. Instead, have the Training Session in the morning or afternoon when your children are more receptive to learning.

Then make the Training Session fun. A Training Session involves role playing and pretending. Kids are acting out the good behavior and they love to do this.

Training Sessions don't have to be long. In fact, if you're training young children, make them short—but do remind them of the correct behavior frequently.

There are eight parts to a Training Session:

1. Give specific instructions with a demonstration.
2. Inform your children of the exact consequence they will receive for not performing the correct behavior.
3. Ask questions to make sure the correct behavior is understood.
4. Practice the correct behavior.
5. Praise the correct behavior.
6. Supervise and inspect to make sure the right behavior is carried out.

7. Enforce any consequence incurred.
8. Review the rules often or as necessary.

To illustrate, let's use the simple example of training your children to rinse off their dishes after a meal.

Remember, the first rule of a Training Session is to schedule it at a neutral time. So if you're training your children to rinse their plates after a meal, plan the Training Session in the morning or afternoon, not during mealtime.

Here's a detailed example of the 8 parts of a Training Session:

1. Give specific instructions with a demonstration.

The first thing you do during a Training Session is to give your children verbal instructions telling them exactly what you want them to do. Be very specific. Tell them what they should AND should not do. Then, demonstrate the correct behavior.

So, when training how to rinse off their dishes after a meal, show your children exactly what to do. Do you want them to use a sponge when rinsing off their plate? Where should they set the plate when they're finished? In the sink? Beside the sink? Where should they put their silverware and glass? Demonstrate exactly how you expect it done.

2. Inform your children of the exact consequence they will receive for not performing the correct behavior.

Having a pre-planned consequence is great for both the parent and children. For the parent, you'll be able to calmly and rationally dispense the consequence since you've already planned it out. For the children, they'll know exactly what's going to happen to them if they break the rules. Getting the consequence will be their decision. If they choose to disobey, they choose to receive the consequence.

For our dish rinsing example, the consequence for leaving their dishes on the table might be that they have to wash off everyone else's dishes at the next meal.

3. Ask questions to make sure the correct behavior is understood.

Ask questions like, "Where are you supposed to set your plate after you've rinsed it off? Where do you set your silverware? What is your consequence for forgetting to rinse off your dishes?"

4. Practice the correct behavior.

Have your children practice carrying in their dishes. Have them practice rinsing off the dishes with the correct sponge and setting them in the right spot.

5. Praise and acknowledge correct behavior.

Be sure to get excited and give lots of praise when they do the task correctly.

6. Supervise and inspect to make sure the good behavior is carried out.

Supervision and inspection are key. Your children need to know that you will definitely be checking that they did what they were supposed to do. So when training to rinse off their dishes, always inspect to see that they did indeed carry in their dishes and rinse them thoroughly.

7. Enforce any consequence incurred.

Enforcing the pre-determined consequence is one of the most important elements of training. For training to be effective, you must follow through with your word. No need to warn them—you already did in the Training Session. So the *first* time they ever leave their dishes on the table, enforce the consequence. Make them carry in and rinse off everyone's dishes. If you consistently follow through on consequences, the poor behavior will eventually be extinguished.

8. Review the rules often.

Before each meal is over, remind your children exactly what to do with their dishes. Be sure to remind them of the consequence for leaving their dishes on the table too.

Review the Rules Often

It's amazing how simply reviewing the rules before a certain activity takes place will help children remember to do the right thing. If you wait until they're screaming or being wild, it really won't have much effect. So *before* you go anywhere or do anything, go over the correct rules of behavior. Be sure to also mention what consequence they will get if they break a rule.

For instance, if you go to the store, before you ever get out of your car, prepare your children how to behave. Your conversation might sound like this: "Remember how you are supposed to behave in the store. I want you to stay right beside me the whole time. Do not wander away from me. Remember also, you are not allowed to throw a fit. If you do, I will immediately take you out to the car and _____. (Name a specific consequence of your choice.) Now, let's review. Are you going to wander away from me? Are you going to throw a fit? What's going to happen if you throw a tantrum in the store?"

Get into the habit of reviewing correct behavior before every activity. Review how you expect your children to act at bedtime, mealtime, playtime, clean-up time, etc. By hearing and practicing right behavior frequently, good behavior will soon become a way of life.

Be Specific

When training your children, be sure to give specific instructions on the correct behavior. For instance, instead of giving a vague, general statement such as, "Be good in the store," you need to tell them specifically what 'being good' means. Can they touch things—or not? Do they have to stay right beside you—or not? Can they ask you to buy them something—or not? Spend a few minutes instructing them in exactly what they may and may not do.

Be an Authority

In order to train your children in correct behavior, you must have authority over them. Why would they obey you if you have no authority? Many parents, however, are hesitant to show authority over their children. After all, they don't want to appear bossy or controlling. But children don't have the maturity or knowledge to know what is truly good for them. They need loving parents to guide them to do the right thing, whether they want to or not. Besides if you don't take control, your children will. That's human nature. Someone invariably takes control when no one else does.

Beyond that, children need to know how to deal with authority. Throughout life, they will encounter all types of authority figures—teachers, principals, policemen, and employers. Children need to learn to obey, respect, and yes, submit to authority, or they'll have trouble coping for the rest of their lives. Imagine a child who has never been taught to yield to authority going to school. What's going to happen when he grows up and has to do what his boss says?

Children don't resent authority from a loving parent. Quite the opposite is true. They love to be taken care of by a strong, confident leader. It gives them a great deal of security. Throughout my years of teaching, I have seen classrooms where the teacher had no control. The children were scared and confused. Children like having someone in charge who can enforce the rules.

Parenthood is not about being best friends with your children. Being a parent is about raising children who will become moral, responsible adults. Once that has been accomplished, then the friendship will come. But in the beginning, the parent must be the authority in order to produce that moral, responsible adult. Besides, kids will have plenty of friends, but only one set of parental figures.

Sample Bedtime Training Session

In this example, let's say you're having a problem with your children resisting going to bed and then constantly coming out of their room after you've tucked them in.

Sit down with your children and let them know that from now on, when you tell them to go to bed, they need to do these four things:

1. Stop what they're doing.
2. Look you in the eye.
3. Say "Yes Mom or Yes Dad" with a good attitude. (Note: See Chapter 5 to learn how to train your children to respond to your instructions.)
4. Immediately get up and start getting ready for bed.

Tell them they need to take a bath, brush their teeth, and go to the bathroom one last time. Then, they're going to get in bed.

Now once they're in bed, they're not allowed to get out of bed. They're not allowed to yell for you or bother you in any way. Let them know that the only way they can call for you is if they're throwing up or bleeding.

Then, let them know the exact consequence they'll receive for not following the rules. And be sure to ask questions along the way, like:

- So what are you going to do when I tell you to go to bed?
- Are you allowed to get out of bed after I tuck you in?
- Can you yell for me if you have a question?
- What is your consequence if you don't obey?

Once you've explained exactly what they're supposed to do, have them practice the correct behavior. Go to the living room, and put a toy on the floor. Have them pretend like they're playing with the toy. Then say, "It's time to get ready for bed." They need to immediately stop, look you in the eye, say "Yes Mom or Yes Dad" with a good attitude, then get up and head toward the bathroom.

Once they're in the bathroom, have them pretend to take a bath, pretend to brush their teeth, and pretend to go to the bathroom. Then, have them get in bed, kiss them goodnight, and leave the room.

Then, do it again! This time have them pretend to be watching TV. When you say it's time for bed, have them repeat the above steps.

Make sure they know exactly what to do that night. You might even want to practice it again in the afternoon. Then, sometime before bedtime, remind them of the rules of bedtime. Ask questions like:

- So what are supposed to do when I tell you to go to bed?
- What is your consequence if you don't?

After that, all you should have to do is simply remind them of the rules each night before bedtime. For the first week or two, be sure to supervise and inspect that they are indeed doing what you trained them to do. If they dawdle, and are not in bed at the specified time, make them start getting ready 30 minutes earlier the next night. And finally, don't forget to give the predetermined consequence if they disobey.

3
TRAINING YOUR CHILD'S HEART

Training is the key to having well-behaved children. There are two distinct parts to training children: training their behavior AND training their hearts. To have well-behaved children, you need to do both. The added benefit of training your children's hearts is that it makes training their behavior a whole lot easier!

Training your child's heart simply means to instill morals, values, and virtues such as kindness, unselfishness, and self-control. In other words, instill a moral code of right and wrong. The goal is to train your child's conscience to do the right thing, even when no one is watching. Training the heart is also referred to as moral training or character development.

By training your children's hearts, you'll improve their overall behavior. Because once you've instilled a strong foundation of what is right and what is wrong, children will begin to do what is right on their own. For instance, once your children know in their hearts the right thing to do is to obey their parents, you won't have to spend as much time on outward compliance.

Training their hearts will also improve children's intellectual, social, and psychological development. For instance, without moral conduct, intellectual development will be delayed. Why? Who do you suppose is going to learn more? Children with self-control who patiently listen to their teacher and do what is expected? Or children who have no self-control, cannot sit still in their seat, and have never been taught to listen and obey. The same goes for social development. Children who are nice and kind generally have many more friends than those who are selfish and unkind. And for those parents who are concerned with their children's psychological development, children will be far healthier emotionally if you teach them moral behavior.

However, realize that children are not born with a set of good morals or virtues. They must be taught. Think about it: You don't have to teach children how to take away another child's toy, hit, lie, or throw a tantrum when they don't get their way. That all comes very natural to them. What doesn't come natural is how to share, be kind, and be unselfish. This comes after much parental training.

Be aware however, if you don't teach your children values, someone else will. But they probably won't be the values you want them to hold. Your children will learn their values from TV, movies, video games, and other kids at school. So for these reasons, parents need to deliberately and actively teach their children right from wrong, and teach the virtues that will make them kind, unselfish, responsible adults.

Start Training the Heart at an Early Age

There's an old story about a mother who asked an expert on moral training when she should start moral instruction with her 5-year-old. The expert responded, "You haven't started? You've already lost five of the most important years."

To build a strong foundation, start moral instruction early. It's been said that 85% of a person's character is formed by age six and by age twelve, it's hardened in stone. I don't know how true that statement is, but I do know the earlier you start teaching morals and virtues the better. Just like languages are learned best when children are young, so is morality and learning how to deny impulses with self-control.

Start moral instruction when your children first begin to understand words, around 6 to 8 months of age. However, if your children are older and you haven't done this yet, don't panic. Despite what you might think, teenagers are capable of learning.

The Three Parts to Training a Child's Heart

So how exactly do you instill morals and virtues? There are three parts to training a child's heart and they must be done in combination:

1. Parental example
2. Instruction
3. Not allowing bad behavior

For instance, if you want your children to be kind: 1) Model it. 2) Teach them how to be kind. 3) Don't allow them to be unkind.

Parental Example

The first part to training a child's heart is through example. Pastor Joel Osteen says that children are like video cameras with legs. They're recording everything you do. They're recording the type of language you use and the tone in which you speak. They're recording how you treat your spouse and how you treat a store clerk. They're recording how you react to frustration and how you deal with anger. They're recording how you behave in heavy traffic and how you deal with difficult people.

With each recording, your children are learning how to act and react in certain situations. In fact, most children's moral, social, and emotional skills come from watching and then imitating how their parent behaves.

To see how you rank as a model of integrity, ask yourself these questions:

- How do you handle conflicts with other people? Do you yell, insult, or intimidate?
- How do you speak of others in front of your children? Do you cut down and ridicule? Are you negative and sarcastic?
- Do you lie about your child's age to get a cheaper price?
- Do you keep quiet when you receive too much change from a store clerk?
- Do you say thank you, please, and excuse me?

So, I'm not here to preach or judge you in any way. Just be aware that children tend to pattern their lives and behavior after their parents.

Instruction

The second part to training a child's heart is through instruction. Training a child's heart through instruction simply means to diligently teach your child what is right and wrong, and teach virtues such as kindness, unselfishness, and self-control. There are two ways you can instruct your child. The first is through short, casual everyday conversations; and the second is with formal instruction.

Everyday Situations:

Lots of values can be taught and caught in everyday, ordinary situations. Probably the most frequent comment I used to say to my sons throughout the day was, "Be kind to one another. Don't be mean." Or, when they'd have a bad attitude, I'd remind them to do everything without grumbling or complaining. Or when one of my boys was ready to get revenge on his brother, I'd say, "Don't repay evil with evil. Instead, if someone is mean to you, repay them with kindness.

Other comments that I seemed to repeat over and over to my sons were:

- If you don't have something nice to say, don't say anything at all.
- In everything you do, let kindness be your rule.
- Remember to build people up, never cut them down.
- That's not nice. Don't say things like that.
- A soft answer stops an argument but harsh words stir up anger.

These types of comments only take a moment, yet teach children what they should and should not do in that particular situation. By hearing good rules of conduct over and over, soon your children will have good character ingrained in their minds.

Watch for natural opportunities to teach about right and wrong. For instance, if you go to a store, teach your children how to politely hold the door for others. If their grandmother needs help, make them go with you to help. When the school has a food drive, make your children participate. When they're playing with friends, insist that they share and be kind. The point is, if you keep your eyes and ears open, there are opportunities throughout each day to impart important values.

Here's the thing though: Unless you spend time being with your children, you'll miss those golden opportunities to teach morals and virtues. That's where the question of quality time verses quantity time comes in. I've heard the answer is quality time ... and lots of it!

Direct Formal Lessons

The second way you can teach morals and virtues is through direct formal lessons. There are all types of curriculum for teaching character development on the internet. There are also dozens of books about morals and values in bookstores and at the library. In these books are subjects such as what if you found a billfold with the owner's name in it? Saw money at a friend's house? Had a seat when an elderly woman didn't? They are fun to read and will open discussion for you and your child to talk about morals.

Allow me to share how I taught my boys virtues and morals. It was free and took less than 10 minutes per day, and I swear by it. The best way that I found to train my sons' hearts was to read to them every day from *The Book of Proverbs* in the Bible.

The Book of Proverbs is known as the book of wisdom. Wisdom means to know what is right and to do it. And that is exactly what I wanted to instill in my sons' hearts: to know what is right and then do it.

There are so many amazing lessons that Proverbs will teach your children. My favorite lesson is that it's the wise man who listens to instruction. It's the fool who doesn't listen. This lesson runs throughout Proverbs. I love it because once you get this lesson instilled in your children's hearts, when they become teenagers, they'll listen to you. I remember trying to teach my boys something when they were in high school, and I could just tell they thought I didn't know what I was talking about. Their eyes glazed over and they would respond with "Mom, please..." Then I'd say, "Remember, it's a wise man who listens to instruction. It's the fool who doesn't listen." Then they'd suddenly say, "You're right. You're right." It was awesome! I still occasionally use those verses with my grown sons.

Another great lesson that Proverbs teaches is that the mother and father are supposed to discipline their children. It specifically says that if you don't discipline your children, you'll ruin their lives.

This is a great lesson for your children to hear over and over. Then, when you do have to discipline and give a consequence, you can tell them that you have to, or you'll ruin their lives. Again, it's awesome!

I also love that Proverbs teaches children that they should obey their mother and father and listen to their instruction. That's another great lesson that children need to have ingrained in their hearts.

The *Book of Proverbs* teaches basic common sense to lead a successful life and avoid many of life's consequences. It gives practical instruction about common ordinary problems, such as:

- Children, obey your parents.
- Parents, discipline your children.
- Work hard; don't be lazy.
- Be honest; don't lie.
- Take advice.
- Choose good friends.
- Control your temper.
- Control your tongue.
- Be kind.
- Be humble.
- Be generous.
- Don't get into debt.
- Don't drink too much.

Here are three examples of a proverb:

- "A good man hates lies; wicked men lie constantly and come to shame." Proverbs 13:5

- "Lazy people want much but get little, but those who work hard will prosper." Proverbs 13:4

- "Listen to counsel and accept discipline, that you may be wise the rest of your days." Proverbs 19:20

Each proverb will give you lots of opportunities to discuss morals, values, and virtues.

So, this is how I did it: I read to my sons each day out of *The Living Bible* translation, but you could use any version that you think your children would understand. I recommend *The Living* or *The Message* version.

I would read one chapter of Proverbs to my sons each day. It would take about 5 to 10 minutes. As I would read, when I'd come to a part that I thought had a good lesson, I would stop and talk about it to make sure they fully understood it.

I started reading Proverbs to my boys as soon as they turned 4 years old and I tried to read a chapter of Proverbs a day until they were about 12. Since I read to my boys every day anyway, I just got into a habit of reading a Proverb first, discussing it, and *then* reading their fun picture or chapter book.

Now be forewarned: These proverbs are difficult for children to understand. That's why you need to stop along the way and explain. However, as your children hear the same proverbs over and over, they'll soon learn to understand them. There are 31 chapters of Proverbs—one for each day of the month. As soon as I finished all 31, I started over.

Now if you're thinking that this is unrealistic and that your children couldn't possibly sit still and listen to Proverbs for 10 minutes, let me give you two thoughts.

My first thought is from the perspective of a teacher. If your children can't sit still and listen for 10 minutes, how do you think they're going to function at school? Maybe that's a sign that you should work on that skill. Have them practice sitting and listening to you read. The more they practice, the longer your children can sit still and listen. I used to read to my boys for at least 30 to 60 minutes at a time when they were two years old. But I did it every day, so they had developed the skill of sitting still and listening.

My other thought is from the perspective as a parent. When you're forcing them to sit still and listen to you read from Proverbs, you're developing many important character traits, such as patience, attentiveness, and self-control. Isn't developing these types of virtues what you're trying to accomplish?

Don't Allow Bad Behavior

Finally, the third part of training a child's heart is not allowing bad behavior. If you're trying to teach honesty, don't allow him to lie. If you're trying to teach respect, don't allow him to be disrespectful. You stop the bad behavior by giving an unpleasant consequence. (See Chapter 9 for consequences.)

Make a Written Plan of the Virtues You Want to Teach

When it comes to training your child's heart, don't leave it up to chance. Have a game plan. You wouldn't build a house without a blueprint. You would carefully plan down to the last detail. Raising your child is far more important than building a house. You need to have a conscious plan of how you want your child to turn out.

Get with your partner and make a list of all the morals and virtues you want to teach your child. Then make a written plan as to how you intend to impart these values. The plan might involve bringing up these character traits in a natural conversation. Or, you might want to have a more systematic approach where you formally teach each character quality. Either way, having a plan will just make you more aware of the morals you want to teach. (See Chapter 4 for Virtues to Teach.)

Guarding Your Child's Heart

In addition to training your child's heart, you also have to guard your child's heart. Children today are being bombarded with inappropriate values. Movies, TV, the internet, music, magazines, and video games are all exalting values that are opposite to most parents' beliefs.

It is imperative for parents to examine what their children watch and listen to. Make sure they reinforce the values you are teaching.

For instance, on most shows, premarital sex is the norm. Do you want your children to think this is the usual dating ritual? When your children watch stuff like this day after day, it becomes ingrained in their heads. They'll soon believe that this is the normal, acceptable way to live, and that your morals are old-fashioned. Why let them fill their minds with values that directly contradict those you are teaching?

Examine all the media to which your children are exposed. If they are not reinforcing and encouraging your morals, don't allow your children to watch them.

The teaching of morals and virtues is a gradual process, not something you teach in an afternoon. So be diligent. Moral lessons learned in childhood stay with us as habits of the heart for the rest of our lives.

4
VIRTUES TO TEACH

While researching to write this chapter, I discovered there are at least 49 virtues to teach your children! For the sake of brevity, I've selected 7 virtues I believe are the most important and will naturally overlap the other virtues. For instance, if you train your children to be kind, they will naturally be compassionate, considerate, generous, friendly, forgiving, helpful, patient, and tolerant. Here are my picks for the top 7 virtues to teach your children.

Self-Control

One of the most important virtues to teach your children is self-control. It is the mother of all virtues because you can't have the other virtues unless you first have self-control. For instance, you can't always be kind, or unselfish, or full of integrity unless you first have the self-control to exhibit those traits.

Self-control, also known as self-discipline or will power, is the ability to control your impulses, emotions, or desires. In other words, self-control means doing the right thing whether you feel like it or not. Whether it's holding your tongue when someone is rude or doing your chores when you'd rather be playing, self-control involves not getting your way and not getting upset about it.

Self-control is needed in every aspect of life. Children (and adults) need self-control to be able to:

- Sit still and listen.
- Control their temper and tongue.
- Persevere to get their work done.
- Respect others and their belongings.
- Stay healthy, by way of diet and exercise.
- Resist overspending.
- Manage internet surfing and gaming.
- Stay drug, alcohol, and smoke free.

A 2005 University of Pennsylvania study showed that self-discipline is twice the predictor of school success as is intelligence. As a teacher, I know this is true—not only in school, but as an adult too. Throughout my teaching career, I've seen incredibly gifted students who fell far short of their potential due to the lack of self-control. They didn't have the self-discipline to study or do what their employers told them to do. Yet I've had lots of students with average intelligence who became very successful. These students knew how to persevere when the assignment got tough and do what was expected.

Children (and adults) who lack self-control have the following traits:

- Self-centeredness
- Laziness
- Disrespect
- Distraction
- Inability to deal with frustration
- Need for instant gratification
- Sense of entitlement
- Addictions

While self-control is one of the top virtues to have, parents often do little in the way of developing it. In fact, unknowingly, parents do things in direct opposition to the development of self-control. Instead of teaching their children they don't always get everything they want in life, these well-intentioned parents believe it is their duty to make sure their kids are always happy. And in their quest to make their children happy, they see to it their children get upset as little as possible.

Here's the problem with that though: In real life, your children are not going to be allowed to get their way all the time. In real life, your children are going to have to do a lot of things they don't want to do when they grow up, like go to work, clean the house, or pay the bills on time. Without the development of self-control, your children will not know how to deal with the frustration of not getting their way or having to do stuff they don't want to do. This is going to make for very unhappy children—and adults.

One way to inhibit the development of self-control is to condition your children to always get their way. For instance, if you tell your child to turn off his video game because his time limit is up, but he gets really upset and doesn't want to, what should you do? Does it really matter if he plays another hour? It's not worth making him upset … is it? But by allowing him to continue, how is that developing his self-control? How is that training him that when he doesn't get what he wants, he needs to accept it with a gracious attitude? Or how about the child who throws a tantrum because he can't have a cookie? When the Mom gives in so she won't upset her child, how does that teach him he won't always get his way?

Somewhere in the past thirty years, parents have gotten it into their heads that they need to satisfy their children's every desire. They think they are terrible parents if they make their children upset or have to wait for something. But giving in constantly just to avoid upsetting your children, teaches neither patience nor restraint nor economic responsibility.

In his book *Emotional Intelligence,* Harvard University professor Daniel Goleman found that children who learn how to delay gratification develop self-control. However, children who were raised to receive immediate gratification as preschoolers grew up to be troubled adults. They were more prone to frustration and anger. And they still expected immediate gratification. In comparison, children who could delay gratification as preschoolers coped better with frustrations and temper issues as adults.

Twenty plus years ago when I was raising my sons, many parenting "experts" advised that parents should let their children vent their anger. I recall reading, "If you don't allow your child to vent his anger, where will his anger go?" I remember thinking, "It will develop his self-control, that's where it will go!" Now I discover there's evidence to back me up. Researchers have found that venting your anger to make you feel better is one of the worst strategies. In fact, outbursts of rage pump up the brain's arousal system, leaving you angrier, not less.

Self-control doesn't happen naturally. It must be developed; and the way to develop it is through practice and repetition. Just like with a skill or talent, the more children practice self-control, the better they'll be at controlling themselves. Here are some ways you can help your child develop self-control:

1. Be a good example. Do you yell and scream when you get mad? Do you lose your temper when you discipline your children? Be aware that your children are learning from you how to act and react in difficult situations.

2. Have a Training Session to train your children how to have self-control. Practice different scenarios about what they should and should not do. Practice: What would you do if you really wanted to do something and I said no? What would you do if you were mad and I sent you to your room? Train them how they should calmly react to frustrations and disappointments.

3. Never reward a temper tantrum. Whatever your children are having a tantrum about, make 100% sure they don't get it! (Note: For young children, you can often prevent tantrums by making sure they have scheduled meals, snacks, and naps.)

4. Start developing self-control early. Even children as young as one should not be allowed to throw a frustration tantrum when they don't get their way. Say something like, "You may not act like that. I'm going to count to three and if you are still crying, I'm going to take you to your room." And then follow through! This teaches that no means no, and they need to learn to deal with not getting their way. I am, of course, not talking about being cold-hearted and mean to your children. I'm suggesting that when they don't get their way on an issue in which you have said no, you don't allow them to act out of control. (Note: This does not apply to children who are crying because of a physical ailment, such as hunger, teething, earache, etc.)

5. Don't allow your children to scream and throw fits or get mad and slam doors. Calmly, but firmly, tell them that those types of behaviors are unacceptable, no matter how mad they are. Inform them of the exact consequence they will receive if they

act out of control, and then be sure to follow through!

6. Delay gratification. Don't give your children everything they want just to avoid conflict. Learning to wait patiently for things develops self-control.

7. Give your children strategies to try when they get upset. Options might include calmly taking a deep breath, counting to 10, or going to another room to cool off.

8. Make your kids do chores. Chores are a great way to develop self-control. Whether it's helping clean up the kitchen each night or cleaning the bathrooms each weekend, chores teach children that in life you've just got to do stuff you don't want to do.

9. Don't allow your children to react angrily and have a bad attitude when they get disciplined. Self-control means having a respectful attitude even if you're upset.

10. Read aloud to your children. Forcing your children to sit still and listen helps develop their self-control, patience, and attentiveness.

11. Require your children to stay quietly in their beds once they've been tucked in. Having them stay in their beds even when they don't want to, helps develop their self-control.

12. Don't be afraid to make your kids do stuff they don't want to do. They will definitely need that skill as an adult.

13. Let your children know they can indeed control their emotions and reactions. It's a skill that can be learned.

A Thankful Heart

Right up there with self-control is having a thankful heart. It's often said thankfulness is the secret to contentment. When people focus on what they do have instead of what they don't have, it totally changes their perspective on life.

Several years ago, I had a student named Jenna. Before the school year even started, all of her former teachers came to my room, put their arms around me and said, "We heard you have Jenna this year. We're so sorry. She's a nightmare."

They told me how Jenna's mother had died three years earlier and she was mad at the world. They said she threw constant tantrums, and would always scream, "You don't understand! My mother is dead!"

The first day of school Jenna was true to form and threw several loud and disruptive tantrums. At first, I tried to be very sympathetic and understanding, but she was out of control. She could only see one thing in her life—her mother died. That was her one and only focus.

So, the next day, I gave her a Gratitude Journal. I told her that instead of the usual morning work, her assignment was to write 10 things she was thankful for. She immediately threw the journal against the wall and screamed, "I don't have anything to be thankful for. My mother is dead!"

I said, "Are you in a wheelchair? Then write down you're thankful you have two healthy legs. Are you blind? Then write down you're thankful for good eyesight. Do you live under a bridge? Then write down you're thankful you have a home."

The first week I had to prompt her on every single thing. She literally couldn't think of anything good on her own. After a while though, she could easily think of 10 things to be thankful for. This assignment forced her to look around and look for the good and not focus on the bad.

Jenna still had her ups and downs that year; but overall, she wasn't bad. The cool thing about this story is, by the next year, Jenna had totally changed. Her new teacher had no idea how disruptive she'd been only the year before. As far as the new teacher was concerned, Jenna was a well-behaved and loving girl. Wow—being thankful had totally transformed her personality.

My mother is another incredible example of how having a thankful heart will give you a positive outlook on life. My mother, age 90, has been a widow AND blind for the last 17 years. She lives alone, rarely gets to go anywhere, and yet she has such a thankful heart. Every time I talk to her, she constantly talks about all her blessings. She says things like, "We're so lucky to live in America where we can take a hot shower every day. Can you imagine not being able to shower every day? We're so lucky!" Or she says, "It's a great time to be blind! I'm so lucky there are so many books on audio now!" Even though most people would be extremely depressed in her situation, my mother is quite content. She has learned to focus on her blessings, and not on what she lacks.

We need to train our children to have a thankful heart so looking for the good will become a habit. Here are a few ideas on how to instill a sense of gratitude:

1. Model thankfulness. Be sure to say things like, "We're so lucky

we live in such a nice house." Or "We're so blessed to live in America where we have so much food. You know a lot of people in the world don't have enough to eat." Start focusing on all your blessings and point them out to your children.

2. Always say thank you. Let your children observe you say thank you to your spouse, to store clerks, to waitresses, and to others. Always tell whoever cooked dinner how much you appreciate their hard work. Insist that your children say thank you for everything as well.

3. Keep a Gratitude Journal either as a family or individual. Challenge your kids to find 10 things each day to write in the Gratitude Journal.

4. Take your children to a poorer area. Sometimes children don't realize how lucky they are until they go somewhere else. I remember on one vacation with my boys how we drove through several really poor little towns. My boys were shocked that the houses were so small and run down. Suddenly our mid-size house was looking pretty good to them.

5. Compare your situations to others in poorer countries. I love the story about the homeless man who was complaining to a new immigrant that he had to sleep in his car. The immigrant was shocked. He said, "You have a car? You must be very rich." No matter what your circumstance, someone somewhere has it worse.

6. Insist that your children write thank you notes for gifts. If your children are too young to write, have them draw a thank you picture and you can write the words for them. Or, at least have them call the gift bearer and tell him thanks in person.

7. Play the Glad Game. I love the old Disney movie *Pollyanna*. In the movie, Pollyanna always finds the good in any situation with the Glad Game. The rules are that no matter what happens, you have to find something to be glad about.

8. Have your kids buy their own nonessentials, such as toys, video games, accessories, etc. When they see how long it takes to save up for things, they'll appreciate them much more.

9. Have your kids help with household chores, such as cooking, cleaning the kitchen, etc. It will give them a new appreciation for all you do.

Kindness

Kindness is the quality of being friendly, generous, and considerate. It involves empathy and helping others. Children who are kind are better liked and happier than those who have never learned this trait.

Here are some ideas on how to instill kindness in your child's heart:

1. Model kindness in both speech and behavior. Speak kindly to your children, to your spouse, and to everyone with whom you come in contact. Be friendly, helpful, and considerate. For instance, let someone with fewer items cut in front of you in line. Be friendly to store clerks. Volunteer to help someone.

2. Teach your children the old adage: If you don't have something nice to say, then don't say anything at all. This is such a simple statement, yet the wisdom of it is profound! Don't allow your child to speak unkindly to or about others. That includes their siblings, their teachers, and their friends.

3. Teach your children to have gracious speech. One of the best social skills you can teach your children is how to build up and encourage others. Teach them to find something good about the person they are interacting with and comment on it. For example, "I really like your hair. You look so beautiful."

4. Teach your children to help others. Begin by having them help you with household chores. They need to learn that helping others is the kind thing to do, and that it is unkind to make someone else do all the work. Then look for ways they can help others outside the family. Take them with you as you help your elderly relatives. Let them help you prepare a casserole for a sick friend. Have them roll the garbage cans back to the house each week for an elderly neighbor. The point is to get your children into a lifetime habit of helping others.

5. Teach empathy. Ask your children questions like "How would you feel if someone was making fun of you? How would you want other people to treat you if you were in a wheelchair?"

6. Teach them the Golden Rule: Treat others like you would want to be treated.

7. Train your children to be friendly. The best way, of course, is to model friendliness. Let your children see you be friendly to neighbors, store clerks, and waitresses. Teach them how to look people in the eye, smile a big smile, and say hello. If they

know the name of the person they are speaking to, be sure to have them use their name when they say hello—"Hello, Mrs. Smith!" One strategy for making friendly small talk is to have your child notice one nice quality in the other person, and have your child compliment that quality. For instance, "I really like your earrings."

8. Teach generosity. Have your children give a portion of their allowance or earnings to either their church or a charity. If you hear of a need, let your children be involved in giving to that need.

9. Place a high importance on how your children treat others. Do not allow them to be hateful, selfish and cruel to others—and that includes their siblings! Also teach them to treat animals with kindness.

10. Teach your children how to forgive others. Explain to them that no one is perfect and everyone makes mistakes. Ask "Do you want people to forgive you when you mess up? Then you need to forgive others." And don't forget to model forgiveness yourself. Be sure to forgive your kids when they disappoint, and ask for forgiveness when you wrong them as well.

Unselfishness

I just read the most interesting book about how the Amish raise their children. It's called *More than Happy: The Wisdom of Amish Parenting* by Serena Miller. While researching the Amish for her fictional novels, Miller noticed that Amish children were incredibly well-behaved, polite, and happy. She was so awed by their behavior, she decided to write a book about how the Amish raise such obedient, contented children.

Among other things, Amish parents teach their children this precept: Their needs are important, but not more important than others. This concept teaches the Amish children that they are to focus on other's needs and not their own. It's all about teaching them to be unselfish!

It doesn't take a government study to know that selfish people are some of the most miserable people around, while unselfish people tend to be a whole lot happier.

If you want your children to become adults of value, teach them how to be unselfish. Here are some ways to develop the trait of unselfishness.

1. Model unselfishness. Let your children see you put the needs or wishes of others before your own.
2. Instill an attitude of helpfulness. Insist your children help you around the house. Encourage them to help relatives and neighbors too.
3. Love your children and give them plenty of attention, but don't allow them to think the world revolves around them.
4. Start teaching unselfishness early. Children are intrinsically self-centered. When your baby or toddler takes away another child's toy, say something like, "No. You must share your toys. You must be kind."
5. Don't overindulge your children with the latest and greatest toys and gadgets. Teach your children the difference between a need and a want. Spoiled children are not happy children.
6. Focus on being helpful and thoughtful toward others. As a family, think about what you could do to be a blessing to others and then do it. There are all kinds of service projects who need volunteers both at local churches and in the community. One of the best places to find needs, however, is right in your own neighborhood. Is there an elderly widow who needs help raking her leaves or shopping? Is there a single mom who needs help with her kids?
7. Teach your children to put themselves in someone else's shoes. Statements like, "If that happened to you, what would you like other people to do for you?"
8. Be sure to praise unselfish acts. When you see or hear your child being thoughtful and considerate to others, be sure to remark on it.
9. Practice hospitality. Have your children help host a dinner or party and teach them to put their guests' needs first.

Integrity

Integrity is the quality of being honest, keeping your word, and consistently doing the right thing, even when no one is watching.

The best way to teach integrity is to be a model of integrity yourself.

Your children need to see that you are always honest, you never lie, and you keep your word.

Then, don't tolerate lying or dishonesty—even in small matters. I once taught with a woman whose daughter I frequently saw. We all knew this girl to be sneaky and deceptive. She would blatantly lie to her mother and her mother would rarely do anything about it. For instance, one day she told her daughter to stay out of the candy. When her daughter came in with chocolate all over her face, the mother asked, "Did you eat that chocolate?" The girl replied, "No." Her mother just shook her head and went on.

That little girl is 30 years old now. She still lies and has a real problem with dishonesty.

Contrast that to my son Hunter. Boy, if Hunter lied, he was in trouble! One time in 7th grade, Hunter lied and we found out. My husband grounded him until he had completely memorized 26 scriptures about lying and honesty. If he messed up once while reciting the verses, he had to wait a day and then start all over.

It took Hunter a couple of weeks to memorize them. But I tell you, Hunter grew into a man of integrity! He is one of the most honest young men you'll ever meet!

Be careful though when getting your children to tell you the truth. If they know that they will be severely punished for telling you what really happened, what incentive is there to tell the truth?

I always told my boys that if they would tell me the truth, they would only get a small consequence. However, if they told me a lie and I found out, they would get a huge consequence.

Here are three ways to encourage integrity:

1. Be a model of honesty and integrity yourself. Never lie or be dishonest and obey the speed limits. (Ouch, that last one is going to be hard!)
2. Keep your word, even if it's hard or inconvenient. Teach your children their word is their bond; and if they say they will do something, they must do it.
3. Do not tolerate lying, even if it's a small matter. Lying is habit forming. Explain the dangers of lying and how it ruins your reputation. Even if you sometimes get away with lies, you eventually get caught. Tell them the story of "The Boy Who Cried Wolf." Once you lie, people no longer believe you, even

when you tell the truth.

Respect

Respect is behaving and speaking in a way that gives people dignity and honor. Children need to learn to have respect for their parents, others, authority, the elderly, and themselves.

Here are some tips to teach respect:

1. Model respect by being respectful to your spouse. How do you treat your spouse? Husbands, do you respect and honor your wife? Wives, do you respect and honor your husband? If you routinely call your spouse (or ex) names or cut them down in front of your children, it will lessen their respect for the other parent. Even snide comments like, "Daddy doesn't do a very good job cleaning you up," can undermine their respect for their father.

2. Try to build up your spouse in the eyes of your children. Say things like: "I bet Daddy can fix your toy. He's so smart!" Or "We're so lucky to have Mommy. She takes such good care of us!"

3. Teach respect with a Training Session. Wait until all is calm, not when disrespect is taking place. Then train your children how you expect them to speak respectfully to you.

4. There should be zero tolerance for disrespect and sass. No matter how angry your children are, it is never an excuse for being disrespectful. Disrespect for a parent is definitely an action that calls for a consequence. In the long run, your children will have more respect for you if you don't allow disrespect.

   However, do open the doors of communication. Let your children know they may disagree with you, but never to speak disrespectfully to you. Tell them if they speak with respect, you will be glad to listen, carefully weigh their point of view, and if appropriate change what you can. However, once you've made a decision, they are not to argue any more about it. You are in charge, and you make the final decisions.

5. Don't allow negative body language. Rolling the eyes, slamming doors, pouting, and dirty looks are nonverbal

messages, but they convey disrespect. Banish them to their room and tell them when their attitude is more respectful they may join you again.

6. Be sure to teach respect for you at an early age during the toddler years. If young children do not respect their parents, they certainly will not develop it during adolescence. As part of the training process, require eye contact when you are speaking. Don't allow them to look down or at the wall. Have them look you straight in the eye as a matter of respect.

7. Demand respect when your children are little, but earn their respect as they grow up. If you want your children to continue to obey you as an adolescent and to accept your values, you must earn their respect. Your children need to admire you enough to believe what you say and to accept that you know what is best for them.

8. Remember, you are their parent, not their friend. Your kids already have plenty of friends, but only one set of parents.

9. Teach your children to have respect for authority. Be a great example by speaking highly of their teachers and law enforcement and expect your children to do the same. If you do have a criticism about their teacher, please don't say it in front of your children. Say it privately to the teacher herself. Make sure you teach your children how to speak respectfully to policemen too. (No calling them pigs or complaining about their speed traps   in front of the kids!)

10. Teach your children to be respectful to their elders. (An elder doesn't necessarily have to be old, just an adult.) Teach them how to hold the door for other people, give up their seat to someone older, stand when an adult enters the room, or let an elderly person ahead of you in line. And remember to model these behaviors yourself.

11. Teach your child to respect other's property. Remind your children before you go to someone else's house to keep their feet off the furniture, eat only at the table, and not to touch things they shouldn't. Supervise to make sure they are respecting the other people's home. Respect for others' property includes malls, stores, churches, and schools. Before going anywhere, remind your children how they should treat others' property with respect and care.

Work Ethic

If you want your children to be responsible and successful in life, teach them to work. Having a strong work ethic is the number one trait of a successful person. Research backs this up too. Studies show that hard work will propel a person higher than either intelligence or talent.

Here are things you can do to instill a strong work ethic.

1. Be an excellent role model. When your children see you getting up each day and working hard, they'll know work is a part of life. Tell them about your job and take them with you to work occasionally so they can see firsthand what you do. Have a positive attitude about work too. If your children hear you constantly grumbling and complaining about your job, it will affect their perspective about work.

    Finally, don't work so hard that you neglect your family. Family time should be a top priority, and if work cuts into that time, then the work is out of balance.

2. Make your children do chores. Not only do chores help instill a work ethic, it teaches kids that everyone has to do their part.

3. Insist that your children help you clean up the kitchen each night. Having your kids eat and then run off to play, leaving all the work for mom is teaching all the wrong lessons: selfishness and laziness. It is rude and unkind to leave all the work for one family member. Many hands make light work. Even children as young as four can be trained to help clean up the kitchen.

4. Require your teen to get a summer job. Having a job as a teenager teaches responsibility, punctuality, money management, working with co-workers, dealing with customers, and learning to follow instructions from a boss. Employment also looks great on a résumé or college application.

5. Do everything in moderation. While children need to be taught a strong work ethic, they also need time to play and be kids. But there's plenty of time in the day to do both. Get your kids into the habit of working first, then playing afterwards.

6. Think teamwork. Do housework together as much as possible. Working together is much more fun!

7. Don't do things yourself that your children could do. Yes, you know you could do a job better and faster, but think of chores

as learning opportunities. Train them to do a chore well, and then for the next several years they can do it on their own.

8. Teach your children that a good work ethic involves getting to work on time and going above and beyond what is expected. (Hunter's first boss told him that if he wasn't 10 minutes early, he considered him late!)

9. Don't buy your kids everything. When they have to work to buy what they want, it will motivate them to work.

10. Start early. When your kids are little is when they want to help the most. Have your toddlers help carry in small bags of groceries, fold washcloths, clean up their messes, put away their shoes, carry in plates, etc. Consider buying a child-size broom and dustpan with a brush. Have them sweep the porch or clean up small messes.

11. Encourage your children to be entrepreneurs. Have them start their own business like: pet walking, lawn care, leaf raking, babysitting, dog waste removal, etc. (See my website for my blog: *30 Ways for Kids to Earn Money* at www.theteachermom.tips.)

5
FIRST-TIME OBEDIENCE

To have well-behaved children, you must have a solid foundation of obedience. And true obedience means they obey the first time.

Not only is obedience easier for the parent, it is far better for the child. Just ask any teacher. Most will notice that children who are obedient are generally a happy group. In contrast, those children who are disobedient seem to have a common trait of unhappiness. Who wants to be with someone who hits, throws tantrums, cries a lot, complains, interrupts, and constantly breaks the rules?

In addition, obedient children will perform far better in school. Children who don't obey at home are not going to miraculously start obeying at school. And children who will not obey their teacher (which involves listening and doing their work) will not learn to their full potential.

Many parents are reluctant to make their children obey simply because they feel that it's not that important. After all, what's the big deal if they don't do what you tell them? Is it really that serious that they continue to jump on your bed after you tell them to stop? But if your children are not in the habit of obeying you in small things, do you think they will have a transformation and obey you in big things?

When my boys were pre-toddlers, they would sometimes do things they weren't supposed to do, but truly were no big deal—like getting into our video tape cabinet. It really didn't hurt anything and it kept them entertained. Since it was inconsequential, I thought about ignoring it, but in doing so, I was missing the point. This wasn't about my tape cabinet. This was about teaching obedience. If I didn't expect them to listen to me about the tape cabinet, why should I expect them to pay attention to me when I told them not to touch the stove? I decided early not to think about the importance of my instructions. Instead, I thought of my instructions as *opportunities to train my children to obey.*

Children who have been trained to obey and children who haven't are as different as night and day. Obedient children are a pure joy to be around. Their parents can take them anywhere—to the mall, restaurants, church—and be proud. Home life is peaceful too. Once a solid foundation of obedience has been established, usually the only discipline that is needed is one simple warning.

On the other hand, children who have not been trained to obey can be a nightmare. It's a major hassle taking them anywhere. Friends and family avoid you. Teachers call and complain. And your home life is a constant battleground as you beg and plead for your children to be good.

Training your children to obey is by far kinder and gentler to both you and your children. As a parent, you know what is best for them. You have the experience and wisdom. Children cannot see the hidden dangers that adults know exist—not only physical dangers, but problems that will appear in their personal and emotional lives if certain behaviors are not corrected. Why would you think that a person who has only lived a few short years would know better than you? You have rules and reasons that children cannot even fathom. That is why it is the parent who must guide and direct their children's behavior. But the fact is, you can't guide and instruct if your children do not obey.

In this quest for obedience, I am not talking about being a control freak who dictates every aspect of your children's life. Certainly, children should be allowed personal preferences and decisions. But *in the area of behavior*, parents must have basic obedience so their children will not only know what is right, but will do what is right.

Expect First-Time Obedience

Have you ever wondered why some parents have kids who obey the first time, while other parents have to repeat warnings over and over? It's all in the training!

If your children know that you give multiple warnings, they have no incentive to obey right away. Why should they? They know you won't do anything about it for a while. However, if your children know that they will get an immediate consequence for not obeying the first time, they soon learn to obey without delay.

Parents often have the misconception children can't obey until they've been warned several times. But why would you expect children to obey the fourth time, but not the first? If you expect your children to obey eventually, why not just train them to obey the first time?

Some would argue that first-time obedience is too strict and authoritarian. They contend that parents who want immediate obedience are oppressive tyrants who want to be lord and master over their children. Well, it depends on how you do it. If your motivation is based on love and what's best for your children, then first-time obedience is actually a much kinder approach.

Why First-Time Obedience is Better for Children

The most obvious reason to have first-time obedience is simply for safety. If your children are used to getting 3 or 4 warnings before they obey, what will happen if they are in immediate danger? They're not going to respond instantly to you in a crisis if they're not in the habit of obeying you under usual circumstances.

I witnessed the need for first-time obedience once with a friend. I had gone to the mall with a friend and her daughter—a child who did not have first-time obedience. As we headed back for the car, my friend told her daughter to stop. As usual, her daughter ignored her. By not obeying, she was very nearly hit by a car.

The second reason to have first-time obedience is it creates a much more peaceful home environment. How? By not training your children to obey the first time, you have to constantly harp on them to get them to obey. Since your children know you won't do anything about their disobedience right away, they learn to tune you out until you reach your boiling point. Then, when you become really angry, they obey just in the nick of time. So in order to get your children to obey, you have to become enraged several times a day. And by that time, a parent is often so infuriated, the consequence is much more severe than it would have been had they just given it after the first command.

Take the case of Kelsey. Every night she battles with her son Jack to go to bed. She has to tell him to go to bed over and over before he ever moves. Jack knows from experience that his mother won't do anything until she gets mad. So he just ignores her, continuing with his play, until he sees that she's reached her limit. Only when she gets really furious does he move. He knows just how far he can push his mother before she'll actually do anything. So Jack finally obeys just in time to escape any type of punishment.

Since Jack doesn't move until she yells and screams, Kelsey concludes that it's the anger that is getting Jack to obey. Consequently, she reasons that she has to get irritated and scream at him whenever she wants him to obey. What a terrible environment to grow up in!

But it isn't the anger that is getting Jack to obey. Kelsey's outrage is just signifying that she has reached her limit, and she's actually getting ready to do something about his misbehavior. It is the forthcoming disciplinary action that is getting Jack to obey.

Training your children to first-time obedience is just fairer. The children know exactly what to expect. If they don't obey the first time, they know with certainty there will be a consequence. On the other hand, for parents without first-time obedience, discipline is random. Their children never know what to expect. Sometimes they can get away with things, yet sometimes they can't. It usually depends on the mood of the parent. That's not fair to the children.

My favorite reason to have first-time obedience is that it helps children develop their self-control. As stated in the previous chapter, self-control is the number one virtue to teach. You can't exhibit the other virtues until you first have self-control.

Think about it: Talents, skills, and qualities are developed through practice and repetition. The more you practice, the better you get.

It's the same with self-control. Self-control must be practiced to be developed. First-time obedience requires children to repeatedly practice self-control. Every time your children have to obey the first time when they don't want to, it develops their self-control.

Like practicing for any skill though, the practicing part is not much fun. It's the benefits later on that make all the annoying practicing worth it.

Children love routine, structure, and predictability. First-time obedience is a stable rule that children can count on.

How to Train First-time Obedience

So how do you get your children to obey the first time? The answer is—you train them! You train your children to respond to you immediately as soon as you give an instruction. They don't ignore you, and they don't defy you. They simply obey without delay—and with a good attitude. You can train your children to obey the first time with a Training Session.

Train your children that when you give an instruction, they need to do these four things:

1. Stop what they're doing.
2. Look you in the eye.
3. Say "Yes Mom" or "Yes Dad" with a good attitude.
4. Do what you told them to do.

(Note: You can train your children to respond with whatever wording you want. It might be "Yes Ma'am" or "Yes Sir." Or, "Okay, I'll do it now." Or, "All right—I will." Just be consistent with the wording.)

The reason you want them to look you in the eye and respond is so you know that they've heard you. It's also a matter of respect.

Then, don't forget to tell them that they'll receive a consequence if they don't obey immediately. That's the key to immediate obedience—immediate correction. In other words, if your children don't comply at once with your command, they need to have a consequence right away. It won't take long before they realize that they must obey the first time.

Then practice first-time obedience. Role play different scenarios such as:

- Put your shoes in the closet.
- Put your backpack in your room.
- Don't touch my cell phone.
- Don't stand on the couch.

Make it fun. Make up situations where your kids have to move a lot and make a lot of noise. Then, when you tell them to stop, they have to obey instantly. So have them jump up and down and scream, and then tell them to stop jumping and screaming. Have them run outside and then call for them to come back inside. Each time they need to stop, look, respond, and obey.

For younger kids, do silly things, like:

- Stop that awful noise!
- Stop running through the kitchen!
- Take that underwear off your head!
- Untie your sister and take that gag out of her mouth!

Be sure to give plenty of praise when they immediately obey. But also be sure to give an immediate consequence when they don't obey.

In the beginning of the training process, be especially diligent. For an entire week, devote yourself to train your children to first-time obedience. That means reminding them daily of the rules of first-time obedience. It also means that every single time you give an instruction, you follow through to make sure that your direction is fully carried out.

Expect Complete Obedience

When you give an instruction, expect it to be carried out completely—not half way or just part of the way. For if you let your children get away with partial obedience, the next time, there will be even less obedience. For instance, if you tell your child to pick up his toys and books, and he only picks up the books, this is not complete obedience.

Most children (as well as many adults) will only do as much as they have to. If your children figure out you tolerate partial obedience, what's the incentive to obey completely?

Only Give One Warning

I remember having a parent conference once with a couple who had a very undisciplined 8-year-old. The parents were struggling to get their son to obey. In the midst of the conversation, the father confided, "I warned him and warned him and warned him and warned him and he just wouldn't obey." I remember thinking, "Well, there's your problem." When you are characterized by repeating warnings, children learn to tune you out. They know you won't take action right away. They have learned to identify when you're finally going to do something, so they can quit just at the last moment.

Repeating warnings is a waste of time. You've already told your children what to do. If they don't do it, it is an act of disobedience. They should get a consequence.

If your children are doing something you want them to stop doing, say so once. If they do not stop the misbehavior immediately, then physically make them stop. That may entail taking away what they have, putting them in time-out, or something else unpleasant. The point is, stop the misbehavior. They must learn when you say "No" you mean it, and it is pointless to continue. With a consistent pattern of this type of response, children will soon obey the first time.

If-then Statements

When giving a warning, tell your children specifically what will happen if they don't obey. This is called an if-then statement. "*If* you touch your brother again, *then* you're going to sit in time out." This will cause them to connect their action with the consequence.

If your children break a rule you've been working on for some time, you may not want to give any warning. If, for instance, you have been training your child not to touch your laptop, and he does, say, "You know you may not touch my laptop. You need to sit in time-out."

True Obedience Requires a Good Attitude

True obedience also requires a good attitude. Not only should your children obey immediately, they need to obey politely and respectfully.

There's an old proverb that says, "Train up a child in the way he should go, and when he is old he won't depart from it." Basically, that means that we should train our children to behave as we would want them to act as adults. Do you want your children to have a bad attitude with their teacher? With their boss? Then don't allow bad habits to form with you. Insist that your children respond to you politely and respectfully.

Many parents think there is nothing they can do about their children's attitude. But that's not true! Your attitude is controlled by the will, not the emotions. Therefore, you can choose your attitude. You can either choose to have a good attitude or a bad attitude. It involves using self-control.

Imagine you were in the middle of a huge fight with your spouse. Then, suddenly the doorbell rings and you look out to see that it's your boss. Don't you imagine you could compose yourself pretty fast and open the door with a smile? Of course you could! In the same way, even if children are upset, they can learn to control their anger to respond respectfully.

Children should be taught how to obey politely and respectfully, even if they don't feel like it. This will help develop their self-control.

Train your children to have a good attitude when speaking to you by not allowing a bad attitude. If your children grumble and complain when you give instructions, calmly but firmly tell them that they may not speak to you with a disrespectful, sassy attitude. Give them a clear consequence if they continue. (Depending on the severity of the disrespect, the consequence might be to send them to their room until they can speak to you with respect.)

True obedience hasn't been carried out until the child obeys unhesitatingly and with a respectful attitude.

If Your Child Defies Your Instructions

What if your children pay no attention to your repeated instructions? Consider it a battle that you must win! Ignoring your instructions is simply a deliberate act of disobedience and willful defiance is not trivial. It must be dealt with.

When parents allow their children to defy them, an attitude of disrespect starts to develop. The child reasons, "If I can walk all over them, they must be weak and cowardly." Children don't want to see their parents that way. Also, if you tolerate willful defiance, expect the same attitude of disrespect with their teachers, authorities, and later on their employers. You are not doing them any favor by allowing them to continue.

So exactly what do you do if your children defy your instructions? Take action! Physically get your children to obey. If that means picking them up to put them in their room, removing all technology from their lives, or something else, do it. That is why it is so important to get willful defiance taken care of in early childhood. (My mother would say by the age of two!) You do not want to go through adolescence with children who are in a habit of disrespectful defiance.

I've read that occasionally you should let your children win when they defy you. I disagree. If you let your children win confrontations occasionally, they know that sometimes you give in and give up. It will only make them more determined to win. Willful defiance is not an area you should let your children win at any time.

I'm all for compromise on personal preferences like when to start shaving, wearing makeup, or the length of their hair. However, in the area of outright disobedience and disrespect, the parent should win.

6
THE #1 RULE OF DISCIPLINE: CONSISTENCY

When I was a child, my mother used a discipline technique where she would count to three. If she got to three, and we had not obeyed yet, we would be in big trouble. The funny thing is, between my other five siblings and me, none of us actually remember her getting to three. In fact, I rarely remember her getting to two. We usually stopped whatever mischief we were doing on the count of one. Why? Because we knew, without a shadow of a doubt, that if we disobeyed, we would DEFINITELY be in big trouble. All six of us knew my mother meant business!

The secret to getting your children to obey is to embed in their little heads when you give a command, you mean business! You don't ignore disobedience. You don't give in. You don't give empty warnings. Instead, you GET UP AND DO SOMETHING to make sure your instructions are followed. Your children must be conditioned to know if you say it, you mean it. It's called consistency, and it is essential for successful discipline.

In the case of my mother, she swears she had all of us trained to know she meant business by the age of two. She had followed through consistently when we were pre-toddlers. After that, she simply had to give a warning because we were conditioned to know that my mother would definitely do something if we disobeyed.

Teachers call it 'Put your bluff in early.' Or, 'Don't smile 'til Halloween.' This just means at the beginning of the school year, you have to be extra strict. You have to make sure your students know you won't put up with misbehavior. Once you've got your 'bluff in,' you can lighten up for the rest of the year. It's the same in parenting. Once you get your 'bluff in' and your children are convinced you won't put up with misbehavior, you can lighten up. (That's why it's so important to begin training your children to obey as pre-toddlers.)

How to Be Consistent

Consistency means you have consistent rules with a certainty they will be enforced. There are two parts to consistent discipline:

- Consistent rules
- Consistent enforcement

Are your rules consistent? Do you make your children eat their snack at the table one day, and then let them eat while roaming the house the next? Are the children allowed to stand on the couch one day and then admonished for doing the same thing the next? Are they only allowed one hour of TV a day, and yet you ignore them when they watch much more? Does your spouse have one set of rules while you have another? Inconsistent rules confuse children about what they can and cannot do.

Get with your spouse and establish consistent rules. Make sure you both agree and are both willing to enforce.

Consistency also means that your rules are enforced every single time. Not every once in a while. Not even most of the time. Consistency means you discipline your children *every single time* they disobey. You don't ignore misbehavior or tolerate it. You stop it with whatever means is appropriate for that circumstance. (Although there are certain behaviors to ignore, deliberate defiance is not one of them.) When your children are 100% convinced there will be a consequence for misbehavior, they'll stop acting out.

Being consistent is just a kinder approach because kids love the predictable. They love to know what's going on. That's why they thrive on routine and boundaries. Consistency makes children feel confident and secure. They don't have to worry about what unpredictable thing is going to happen. They know exactly what's going to happen next. They know with great certainty there will be a consequence for breaking a rule.

Inconsistency, on the other hand, confuses children. The children never know what to expect. Will their parents ignore this misbehavior as they've done in the past? Will they just threaten but never really do anything about it? Or, will they actually get a consequence? Inconsistency leaves children feeling anxious and uncertain.

Being consistent doesn't mean you have to use the same consequence each time. You can vary the consequence. Being consistent simply means you always stop the inappropriate behavior.

Some might argue if they punished their children every time they disobeyed, that's all they'd do all day. But that's not true! The beauty of consistency is if you are truly consistent, you won't *have* to discipline your children all the time. Usually a warning will suffice. Like my siblings and me, they'll know if they disobey, they will definitely get a consequence. The misbehavior won't be worth the trouble it causes.

Many parents feel it is just not that important to make children obey every single time. They remember the clichés, 'Don't sweat the small stuff,' and 'Pick your battles.' So these parents decide only to discipline their children for larger issues. While those clichés might be true for some areas of life, it is not true in the area of disobedience. If children will not obey you in small things, don't expect them to suddenly obey you in important matters. However, if you train them to obey in smaller things, they'll be in the habit of obeying for more critical issues.

But what about showing mercy? Everyone makes mistakes, and you need to teach your children to be merciful. That's true, however, when your child has been deliberately defiant and rebellious, that is not the time to show mercy. The time to show mercy is when the child who is usually obedient makes an occasional mistake.

But what about forgiveness? Forgiveness is definitely a quality we need to teach our children. No matter what your children have done, you need to make sure they know that you forgive them. However, for deliberately disobedient children, forgiveness does not nullify the consequence. You need to tell them that you forgive them and that you love them. But you love them so much, you cannot allow them to grow up with a bad attitude, or think they can disregard rules. They still get a consequence.

If you cannot bear the thought of being that strict with your children, think about this: You are not being mean by training and correcting your children. You're being mean when you don't. To allow your children to grow up undisciplined and unable to handle it when they have to follow rules, is not being compassionate. It's cruel. How will they function as an adult? If letting your children get away with things would make them good and responsible, it would be worth it. But it doesn't. It could very well make them unlikable and spoiled. It is much kinder to have your children endure a few moments of tears than to have a life-time of potential heartache.

Besides, your relationship with your children shouldn't center on when you discipline. The majority of your time should be spent loving, encouraging, and up-lifting your children, BUT when they've broken a rule, they should be in trouble. Children who know they are dearly loved will not consider you mean when you enforce the rules. They are just learning that you keep your word.

Children like parents who have rules and confidently enforce them. When children see they can easily manipulate you, they'll have less respect for you. And children who respect their parents will love them far greater than children who have no respect for them.

Supervise to Make Sure Instructions Are Followed

Many common threads connect parents who have well-behaved children. One common trait is that they supervise to make sure their children do what they were told to do. How many times have you seen parents at a store tell their children not to touch anything, and then turn around and totally ignore them? The children, of course, are behind the parents touching everything in sight. Why not? The parents will never know. How could they possibly receive a consequence when their parents are not even aware of what is going on?

If you have a rule or give a command, you must check to see it is fully carried out. If you tell them to stop doing something, don't turn around and never look back. Watch them for a few minutes, and then constantly check to see they really are obeying your rule. If you tell them not to touch something, keep an eye on them. Make sure they really don't touch it. It's especially important to follow up your instructions while your children are young. For once you get your bluff in, and they know that you'll be checking them, you won't have to follow up as much when they get older.

Children Will Test You

Children are concrete thinkers. Sometimes just telling them about a rule and its consequences isn't enough. They must actually experience it. They must see for themselves if you really mean what you say.

Children test everything. They test to see what happens when they open and shut the door. They test to see if the same thing will happen again when they open and shut the gate. That's the way they learn. They learn about their parents in the same way. They will test you. They want to see what mommy will do if they pick up her cell phone. What will she do if they pick up her phone again? By testing their parents, children can discover exactly what they can get away with and what they can't.

If you consistently enforce the rules, and deliver a consequence each and every time your children disobey, they will eventually stop testing you. If, however, your children can even occasionally get away with certain bad behaviors, testing you will always be worth a try.

Even after the initial testing stage, some children will misbehave every once in a while just to see if you're still faithful to your word. It gives children great security to know their world is consistent and their parents are firm and confident.

It's Hard Work!

In the short-term, being consistent takes a lot of time and energy. You have to really pay attention to your children, and make sure they follow through on what you told them to do. You have to check up on them, even when you're busy. You have to see that they obey, even while you're visiting friends. And you have to respond immediately, even when you're dead-tired.

But long-term benefits are immense! Once your children know without a shadow of a doubt that if they misbehave there will definitely be an unpleasant consequence, the misbehavior will come less and less often. Yes, disciplining your children is hard work, but you'll be rewarded for your diligence with well-behaved children.

7
TEN COMMON DISCIPLINE MISTAKES

Mistakes are some of life's best teachers. But if you can learn from the mistakes of others, that's even better! With that in mind, here is my list of the top ten discipline mistakes.

Mistake #1: Failing to Follow Through

There is probably no worse discipline mistake than to make rules or give instructions and then neglect to enforce them. Most parents fall into this trap when they repeatedly warn, threaten, and plead with their children, but don't take any action.

A good example of this is a mother and son I once observed at a meeting. The son was sitting behind his mother and was kicking her seat. She looked back and told him to stop. He kept kicking. She turned around and snapped, "I mean it! Stop kicking my seat!" He continued. Again, she turned around and said, "I'm not going to tell you again! Stop kicking my seat!" He persisted. Then she pleaded. "Joel, please. Don't kick my seat anymore." This saga continued throughout most of the meeting. The boy obviously knew from experience that his mother was all talk and no action.

When you give children a warning or command and then don't follow through to see that's it obeyed, it teaches your children that there's really no reason to comply. Why should they? They can usually ignore you with no consequence. Even if you do follow through some of the time, there's always the chance they can get away with it. It's a gamble, and it's worth the risk. So if you're too tired to move or too busy, then don't say anything at all.

Mistake #2: Giving In

Another major discipline mistake is to 'give in' to whining, nagging, misbehaving children. 'Giving in' simply means that parents let their demanding children have their way just to avoid any conflict. While giving in to your children's tirades may solve the immediate dilemma, it will only create more long-term discipline problems.

Giving in, even occasionally, will keep bad behavior alive. In educational terms, it is known as the "Law of Reinforcement." In regard to children, it means if children get a desirable, appealing response to their behavior, they'll repeat the behavior. In other words, if crying, screaming, pouting, or whining get children what they want, you can bet they'll try this technique over and over again.

For example, imagine a mom and her 3-year-old daughter at a store. Suddenly the 3 year old starts to scream and cry because her mother won't buy her a toy. So to avoid the embarrassment and turmoil, the mother gives in and buys her daughter the toy. Now what does that teach the little girl? It teaches her if she cries and attracts attention, her mother will give her what she wants. You can rest assured the next time they go to the store, the same behavior will happen again; only this time, the child will probably have to cry harder and louder. It will take many more trips to the store without caving in to extinguish that one time the mother gave in.

Every time you give in, expect a repeat of the same behavior—only worse. When parents give in and their children get their demands, it's as if a light bulb appears over their head. These children now have a proven technique of getting their way. It might be begging, whining, pleading, screaming, holding their breath, or throwing a tantrum. Whatever worked for them once will work again.

In fact, most bad behavior which keeps repeating has been reinforced somewhere along the way. Consider Liam. When Liam's mother told him to go to bed, he threw a tantrum. Instead of being firm, his tired, weary mother said, "Okay, you can stay up 30 more minutes." Liam now knows that throwing a tantrum pays. Mia wants a cupcake an hour before dinner. When her mother says no, Mia throws herself on the floor and wails. Not wanting to upset her precious child, the mother gives her the cupcake. You can bet Mia will now throw a fit every time she doesn't get her way. Whatever behavior gets good results, will be repeated. Therefore, it is crucial that you NEVER REWARD BAD BEHAVIOR! That means if your children are behaving badly, make absolute certain they don't get their way.

Stopping a behavior works the same way. Unrewarded behavior will disappear. In other words, if children do not get a satisfying result from their behavior, they'll stop it.. Let's use the previous example of the 3 year old who cried for her mother to buy her a toy. Instead of giving in and thus rewarding her tantrum, the mother could have physically picked her up, taken her out to the car, and given her a consequence. That way the child would have learned that crying and whining for a toy does no good. A note of caution, however: If a behavior has been reinforced in the past, children may try it several times before realizing it doesn't work. Be persistent. It often takes considerable time to undo bad habits.

The Law of Reinforcement works both positively and negatively. To use this law effectively as a parent, never reward bad behavior. Instead, only reward good behavior.

Giving in is only a short-term solution. It may save you from the hassles of the moment, but it can cause a lifetime of problems. Remember, the more you give in, the worse the behavior will be.

Mistake #3: Rewarding Poor Behavior

As stated in the Law of Reinforcement, any behavior that is rewarded or reinforced will be repeated. Therefore, it is imperative you *never reward bad behavior!* While this sounds obvious, I have seen parents do this time and time again.

For instance, take the case of Jessica. She and a friend took her daughter Ava out to eat in a restaurant. She promised Ava that they would get ice cream afterward *if* she was good. Ava was terrible! She broke every rule in the book. When Jessica told her they weren't getting ice cream now, Ava cried and cried. Finally, Jessica said, "Okay, we'll get you some ice cream."

Or consider Amanda. While taking her son Mason to the mall, he asked for a Coke. She told him no. Over and over again he whined for a Coke. Finally, Amanda couldn't stand his whining anymore, so she bought him a Coke. Inadvertently, she had reinforced the very behavior that was driving her crazy. She had just taught her son if he whines long enough, she'll cave in.

So what do you do when your children whine, complain, pout, or throw a tantrum when they don't get their way? First, realize you are in charge, not the children. Simply tell them to stop whining or complaining or pouting or whatever or there will be a consequence. Then, if they continue, send them to their room or give them some other consequence, but don't allow the poor behavior to continue, much less be rewarded.

Mistake #4: Yelling and Screaming

For some parents, yelling and screaming is their main discipline technique. Initially, yelling and screaming may get children to stop the undesirable behavior. However, once the shock of the yelling wears off and they realize there is no action behind your words, yelling is ineffective. They will soon just tune you out. Or, parents discover the only way to get their children's attention is to scream louder and be meaner. As a result, parents have to be irritated most of the time just to get their children to obey.

Among other negatives, yelling gives the appearance that the parent has no control. The angry parent seems frustrated and powerless. When your children see how upset and flustered they can make you, it often becomes fun. Don't play that game. Just calmly take action and be done with it.

Mistake #5: Idle Threats

If you don't intend to fully carry out a threat, then don't say anything. While it may be tempting to tell your dawdling child you're going to leave her at the zoo if she doesn't hurry, would you really? She'd probably love to test you to see if you really would leave her. Unless you truly are planning to abandon her, don't say it.

Many parents don't enforce what they say because they often make unreasonable statements. For instance, in a heated moment, they might tell their child to pick up his clothes immediately or he's grounded for a week. Or, they might say, "Pick up all of these toys or I'm giving them all away." Then, after they think about it, they realize it was an irrational consequence and don't enforce it. If you don't have every intention of enforcing a threat, don't say it.

Mistake #6: Bribing

When I first began teaching in the 1980s, bribing was very popular. Teachers would bribe their students with stickers, Friday movies, pizza parties, etc. in the hope of getting their students to obey. (While the teachers like to call them rewards, essentially they were bribes.) And yes, it often did work. That's why so many teachers did it.

One year when I taught second grade, I had several students who all had been in the same first grade class. Their first grade teacher was a briber! She gave them rewards (or bribes) for everything. What I noticed, though, was these students didn't want to do anything unless I gave them something for it. If I told them to pick up their trash on the floor, they would respond with, "What will you give me if I do it?" It took me a long time to get them to do something on its own merit.

While a bribe usually does work in the short-term, it causes many long-term problems. First of all, bribing teaches children to obey only if there's something in it for them. What a selfish lesson to teach children! The children are not learning to do something because it's the right thing to do. Or, because it would help someone else. Or, because it would show respect to their elders. It only enforces the idea they shouldn't have to do anything unless they get something out of it.

Secondly, the value of the bribes has to be constantly increased. Little bribes soon lose their value, and the bribes have to get bigger and better each time to work. While you may be able to handle this when your children are young, it's going to get very expensive by the time they reach the teen years.

While it is probably okay to occasionally reward your children, know the difference between a reward and bribe. A bribe is promised to the children before they behave correctly. That's how parents get their children to obey in the first place. Rewards, on the other hand, are given unexpectedly, after the children have been good. In other words, the children had no idea they would be rewarded for their good behavior.

Bribes are okay if you want your children to work toward a certain skill such as learning a sonata by Mozart or learning to do a back hand-spring. In this way, it's more of a goal incentive. But don't use bribes to control behavior. Children need to learn to obey because it's the right thing to do.

If you do want to reward good behavior, use words instead of materialistic items. Acknowledge their good works with praise, encouragement, and affection. While an occasional reward is probably harmless, make sure it doesn't become a habitual method of discipline.

Mistake # 7: Allowing Begging

One area that many parents have trouble in is teaching their children that their word is final. These parents let their children continue to beg and plead long after they have said no. The problem with letting children continue their whiney request is that often the parents eventually give in just to stop the nagging. And once the parents give in, it teaches the children that if they continue to plead long enough, they can wear their parents down. The lesson is—badgering pays! Is that what you want to teach your children?

Train your children early that when you say no, they are not to ask again. If they do ask again, they should get a consequence. Once your children figure out that no definitely means no, they won't go through the recurrent ordeal of nagging you.

The Respectful Appeal

While your children need to accept your word as final, they should also be allowed to make an appeal on a decision they believe is unfair. This should be different from just whining and asking again. Train them to say, "May I make a respectful appeal?" In this way, you would know they have a legitimate concern for your decision. Listen carefully to their appeal and weigh their point of view. However, once your decision has been made, they need to accept your answer. That means no whining, pouting, complaining, or slamming of doors. And teach them early that appeals only work when asked nicely and respectfully.

Mistake #8: Unclear Instructions

Often children don't take their parents seriously because of the way parents phrase their instructions. In an effort to be polite, many parents only wish or request that their children do something. For instance, instead of telling their child not to dump all the toys out, they might say, "I wish you wouldn't do that." Or, they turn a command into a question. "How about you clean up your mess, okay?" Now do these types of statements sound like you mean business? While wishing or asking may seem polite, it only confuses children because it sounds as if they have a choice in the matter.

If you want your children to do something, don't wish or ask. Tell them. Say, "Do not dump your toys out." Or, "Clean up your mess now." It doesn't mean you have to be unpleasant or disagreeable. Giving instructions with authority simply means you tell them exactly what you want them to do. This leaves no room for confusion.

Mistake #9: Double Signals

Double signals are given by parents who say one thing, but indicate something else either by facial expression or just a general attitude of apathy. Double signals are often given when the misbehavior is only small or trivial, or when the misbehavior is amusing or cute. The parents know that the children shouldn't be doing it, but they hate to start a conflict over such a minor matter. So without much conviction, they give a command. They hope their children will obey, but they don't insist on it.

A good example of this is when my sons were about 18 months old. They had found my portable cassette radio on the floor. They immediately began to play with it. I said, "No boys. Don't touch." They stopped for a moment, but then continued. I again said, "No.", but since they weren't really hurting it, I never got up. I had said no with my mouth, but yes with my attitude. What I had inadvertently done was to teach my children it was okay to disobey me.

The problem with giving double signals is that when you don't expect your children to obey you every time, they'll become confused about when they do have to obey. When you tell your children no, follow through to make sure that your command is obeyed.

Mistake #10: Thinking Short-term

Last on my list of common discipline mistakes are parents who think short-term. These parents do whatever is easiest for the moment, even if it's not best for the long-term. They buy their screaming child the toy he wants just so they can finish their shopping. They pick up the toys themselves because it's easier than to have a major battle. They want to avoid conflict at all cost, so they look for a quick fix to their problem. But they need to ask themselves these questions:

- Will my response to this problem put an end to this misbehavior, or will it only prolong it?
- Will my response to this misbehavior make my child a good, kind, unselfish person, or am I contributing to forming a spoiled brat?

It's important for parents to do what is best for their children in the long-term. And the best thing is to correct wrong behavior that could keep them from being the best they can be—even if it does cause some sorrow.

Some parents have the mistaken idea they should never upset their children. However, if you do what's best for your children, you can count on them being unhappy some of the time. The reality is, when you have rules and enforce them, your children will not always be happy about it. But rules are necessary.

Good parenting isn't about making your children continually happy. In fact, to do what's best for them will cause occasional short-term unhappiness. But it's much more important to make your children good people than it is to make them temporarily happy. Besides, in the long run, they'll be much happier if they possess the qualities of good, unselfish people. And be realistic. Life is not always happy. You need to teach them how to deal with frustrations and give them skills and qualities to make themselves happy.

Good parenting is not giving children what they want. It's giving them what they need.

8
GUIDELINES FOR GIVING CONSEQUENCES

There are two distinct parts to training children:

1. Instructing and practicing proper behavior.
2. Stopping wrong behavior.

If you can stop wrong behavior with a verbal correction, that's great! For compliant children or children who are already trained to obey, a verbal correction is probably all that is needed.

However, if you cannot get your children to comply with a verbal correction, then a consequence is needed.

Some parenting philosophies say not to use consequences or punishments of any type. Instead, parents are advised to use love, guidance, understanding, and communication.

Sounds wonderful, doesn't it? And when you think about it, it makes sense. The question is: Does it actually work? Can you really stop bad behavior without some sort of consequence?

Because I've seen so many teaching fads which haven't worked, I've grown skeptical about believing every new method that comes along. I no longer unquestionably accept empty rhetoric. I want evidence!

Allow me to give you a brief history, so you'll understand where I'm coming from. I started teaching in 1983. My mother was also a teacher for 30 years, starting in 1968. Together, we have witnessed many teaching trends that have come and gone. Each time, the promises sounded amazing. And these new ideas were great, except for one tiny detail: they didn't work.

For instance, in the 1970s, the United States spent millions of dollars building or converting schools to Open Classrooms. (Classrooms with no walls.) This idea was all backed by research too. It was a disaster! After a few years, schools had to spend millions of dollars putting the walls or partitions back up!

Whole language was another idea that was full of incredible hype. Again, we spent millions of dollars implementing whole language. But again, it was a dismal failure. I could go on and on, but you get my point. Do you understand why I'm skeptical of a lot of rhetoric and promises?

The fact is, I've actually experienced the no-consequence approach. One year, the school where I was teaching decided to implement a positive discipline program that used no consequences. (Oh the rhetoric sounded so awesome!) Instead, we were to resolve any disciplinary problems with daily class meetings. We were encouraged to talk it out and find solutions other than consequences. The entire staff was trained, and we implemented the positive discipline exactly as taught. It was a complete failure! One teacher actually quit the week of Halloween because her students were so out of control! We went back to using consequences the next year.

In addition to trying it myself, I have known several families who have used the no-consequence method. These parents were full of love, understanding, and communication. The results, however, were children who lacked self-control and manners.

Parents have used consequences for centuries because they work. The reason they work is that most people's actions are based on the consequences that follow. If there are no negative consequences for bad behavior, there are fewer incentives to do the right thing.

Think about it. Would you obey the speed limit if there were no speeding tickets? Would you pay the full amount of taxes if there were no penalties? It's doubtful.

People will especially do the right thing if they know that the consequence is *certain*. Children are no different. Children will behave a certain way simply to avoid getting an undesirable consequence.

I understand that most loving parents hate to give consequences. Who wants to upset their precious child? But our job as parents is to prepare our children for the real world. In the real world, life is full of natural, negative consequences for wrong behavior. If you don't pay your bills on time, you get a late fee and a bad credit score. If you don't do what the boss says, you get fired.

Children need to learn early there are consequences connected to their behavior. When children are spared from receiving consequences, they don't learn that consequences follow wrong behavior.

Wouldn't it be kinder for children to learn there are repercussions for bad behavior in a protected, loving home environment? Otherwise, they'll have to learn about consequences as adults where the stakes are much higher.

Children aren't going to suffer any long-term effects from getting a consequence. But they will suffer long-term if they are raised without discipline. It is much crueler to let children grow up unrestrained with no self-control than to give them a consequence when they deserve it. Out-of-control children are likely to grow up to be out-of-control adults. Now that's cruel!

Consequence Guidelines

Consequences are a very effective tool to change bad behavior. However, like any useful tool, if used incorrectly, they can also be harmful. It's very important that consequences are given in love with the purpose of training right behavior.

Following are some guidelines to giving consequences correctly.

Only Give a Consequence When Your Child Intentionally Disobeys

A consequence should only be given when children know the right thing to do, but deliberately don't do it. For instance, if you tell them to stop something, yet they continue, that calls for a consequence. If you have taught them not to go into your office without permission and they do, that calls for a consequence.

However, if children have not been taught that a certain behavior is wrong, there should be no consequence. This is especially applicable to very young children. How would they know that a behavior was wrong if they've never been taught?

So if your toddler squirts toothpaste all over your bathroom, that's not an act of disobedience. That's just childish curiosity. However, once you've taught him the rule about toothpaste and he does it again, then he should receive a consequence.

The best way to determine if your children should get a consequence for poor behavior is simply to examine their motive. Was it an innocent accident or mistake? Then no consequence should be given. If, however, your children knew the right thing to do and willingly chose the wrong thing, a consequence should be given.

Give Consequences with Love

Before my mother ever gave me a consequence, she would always say: "I'm going to discipline you because I love you. If I didn't love you, I wouldn't care how you turned out. I want you to grow up to be well-liked and respected. If I let you be disobedient and undisciplined, that wouldn't be best for you." I always understood that I was disciplined because she loved me.

Whenever you give a consequence, make it clear to your children that you're disciplining them because you love them. It's not because you're mad at them, or that you're mean. You're doing it because if you didn't, they would grow up to be spoiled and out of control. When your children know that you're disciplining them out of love, they won't resent it.

Verbal Correction Should Accompany a Consequence

The whole purpose of giving a consequence is to stop wrong behavior and teach right behavior. Therefore, when you give a consequence, always give verbal instructions as well. Children need to know what they have done wrong, why it was wrong, and what the correct behavior should be.

Remain Calm

While anger may seem to get immediate results, it is much better to let the consequences do the talking. Calmly say, "You broke the rule. I told you that if you broke this rule, then you would get this consequence." Then enforce the consequence. No need to yell, scream, condemn, or ridicule. The behavior will be stopped through the consequence. Not only will your children see that you're in total control, it will also be an excellent example for them to follow.

That's not to say that you will never get angry at your children, because you will. It's unavoidable. But there's a difference between showing irritation and throwing an adult-size tantrum. For instance, if you just told your child not to shoot arrows in the house, and then wham, an arrow breaks your glass door; don't feel guilty for being angry. He just broke your glass door! Being angry doesn't mean screaming and yelling and hitting them. It just means it's okay to give them an intense lecture.

If you become very angry and feel like screaming and hitting, leave the room. Tell your children that you need time to think about their consequence. Give them a specific time when you'll get back with them, and then leave. Don't keep talking. Just get out and calm down. Often the punishment children can conjure up in their mind will be far worse than what you'll dole out anyway.

It's also effective to show empathy when giving a consequence. After all, your children just made a very poor choice and now they're going to get a consequence. You should be sad for them. By showing empathy, you're not the bad guy. You're just following through on what you said you'd do. This will put the burden of guilt on the party who deserves it, not you the parent.

I often would give consequences to my students in my very sweetest voice. I'd say something like, "Oh Ryan, now you're going to have to go back to your seat. You know that if you talk in the game center, you have to sit down." I acted very sad for him that he had made such a poor choice, but I enforced the consequence anyway. As an adult, I had to keep my word.

Give Consequence with Adequate Firmness

The hardest thing for me as a parent was to balance being firm enough so my children obeyed me, yet sweet enough to have a loving environment. There were days when I knew I was being too permissive. Then, there were days when I felt like I was on them all the time. It is truly a difficult balancing act!

In school, I would tell my students that I was the sweetest, nicest teacher in the world when they obeyed, BUT if they disobeyed, I could be downright unpleasant. That became my motto at home. The day was filled with laughter, fun, hugging, and love, BUT, when they disobeyed, I became very firm. The tone of my voice changed and my smile was gone. They had better stop whatever mischief they were in, or there would be an immediate consequence.

If consequences are to stop misbehavior they must be administered with sufficient firmness. If your children repeat the same behavior again and again, that's one sign you weren't firm enough. If your children go away laughing or are totally unchanged, that's another indication you need to increase your firmness. A consequence works when it produces sorrow and a change in action.

Consequence Depends on Age

Obviously, what works on a four-year-old will not work on a teenager. For a four-year-old who just hit his friend, sitting by himself for 5 minutes will upset him greatly. For a teenager who just missed curfew, it might be no car privileges for 2 weeks. You know your children better than anyone. Which consequence will be a real deterrent?

Individualize Consequences to the Child's Temperament

Different consequences work with different children. What works on one child may not work on another. For some children, just a stern look from their parent is enough to send them into tears. For others, verbal warnings have no effect and the children need a much harsher consequence.

My twin boys were a perfect example of this. I only had to scold Skyler, and it would upset him greatly. On the other hand, if I put him in time-out, he was as happy as a clam. He loved to be by himself. Hunter was just the opposite. Verbal reprimands meant nothing to Hunter. But being the socialite that he was, he couldn't stand being in time-out. So tailor your style of parenting and deal with your children according to their temperament.

Make Consequences Known

When possible, let your children know the exact consequence they will receive for breaking a rule. As discussed in Chapter 5, one of the best ways to let the consequence be known is with if-then statements. *If you* throw your toy again, *then* I'm going to take away your toy. Or, *if* you touch your brother again, *then* you'll have to go to your room for 10 minutes. If-then statements simply warn the children exactly what will happen to them if they do the undesirable behavior. Then, if they disobey, you simply carry out exactly what you said you would do. No need to warn again. No need to yell. Just immediately administer the consequence.

When giving if-then statements, make sure you give a specific consequence. Statements such as, "If you touch the TV, then you're going to get it," is too vague. Let your children know specifically what will happen if they misbehave. "If you touch the TV, then I'm going to put you in your room for 5 minutes."

The beauty of making the consequence known before the misbehavior begins is that if your children get a consequence, it was their choice. When they chose to break a rule you have clearly told them not to do, they also chose to get the consequence. They knew exactly what they were doing. If you tell your child that if he throws sand at his brother, then he'll be in time-out; then it's totally up to him whether he gets to play or not. If he gets upset because he has to go to time-out, calmly explain that it was his choice.

Another great strategy is to give your children a choice. In school, if a student was being noisy in the game center, I would say, "Ethan, you have a choice. You may either play quietly at the center where I can't hear you, or you'll have to put your head down at your desk. Which one do you want to do?" This takes the burden off of you. It will be totally up to the children to either behave correctly or get a consequence.

Plan Out Consequences

It's often difficult to think rationally when your children are driving you crazy. It's also easy to lash out in anger and do something you might regret when your children are behaving badly. Therefore, it is important to think ahead while you're calm, and plan how you will handle it when your children break a rule.

Begin by thinking of everyday problems that occur. What would be the best way to get your children to stop a certain undesirable behavior? Write it down if necessary and get input from your spouse. Next, try to predict every foreseeable problem and plan out how you're going to react. By having a game plan, you can calmly and rationally deal with predictable problems.

Another benefit of planning your response to your children's misbehavior is that it will give the appearance of confidence and control. The parents see the problem and can respond immediately. However, when parents aren't quite sure what to do, they often waver on their decision. And when children detect indecision, they often take advantage of the situation. So be prepared and be confident.

Give Consequences in Private

If possible, don't give a consequence to your children in front of other siblings, friends, relatives, or strangers. It's upsetting enough to be in trouble, much less to be embarrassed in front of others. Besides, if you give a consequence in front of others, children will focus more on their humiliation than on what they did wrong.

So, if you're at a store, take them to an isolated corridor, to the car, or outside. If they're with friends, take them to another space. This will also help them avoid trying to save face and further misbehave.

Don't Be Talked Out of the Consequence

Be aware that most resourceful children will try to talk you out of their consequence. Don't buy it. If they did the crime, they need to do the time, no matter how repentant they may seem. Even if they cry and promise never to do it again, say, "I'm so happy to hear that, however, you still have the consequence." If you cancel the consequence every time they cry, you're training them to act repentant even if they're not.

My son Hunter used to manipulate me in that way until I finally caught on. If he broke a rule, he would say, "I'm sorry Mom. Please don't give me a consequence. I won't do it again." I would think he was truly remorseful and not give him the consequence. Within a short time, he would break the exact same rule again and then say the exact same thing. He was confident that I wouldn't discipline him if he promised not to do it again. When I finally started giving him a consequence, even when he was sincerely apologetic, the bad behavior stopped. He finally realized that he couldn't get away with it.

If you reconsider the consequence every time your children are unhappy about a decision, it will make them think they can talk or lie their way out of anything. If they get mad and throw a tantrum trying to avoid the consequence, simply say, "You knew the rules and you knew the consequence. It was your choice. End of argument."

If your children are unhappy with the consequence you've set, remind them they can make one respectful appeal. (See Chapter 7.) However, after you've considered their appeal, they must abide by your decision. It is not your children's place to negotiate the consequence.

9
CONSEQUENCES

The type of consequence you use will depend on the circumstance and the temperament of both you and your children. This chapter will give you several options. If one doesn't agree with you, try another. It really doesn't matter which option you use as long as it stops the unacceptable behavior.

Verbal Correction

With some children, the only consequence needed is a verbal correction. This is especially true if the children are already obedient, or if it's just a minor infraction.

With a verbal correction, you're just calmly telling your kids exactly what they did that was wrong and what they should do instead. For instance, "Boys, don't throw the ball in the house. Go outside to throw the ball."

Logical or Natural Consequences

A logical consequence simply means the punishment should relate logically to the circumstance. If, for instance, a child is throwing blocks, make him put the blocks away. If he dumps the cat food, make him clean it up. If he has trouble getting up for school, make him go to bed an hour earlier. The point is, don't let him get away with poor behavior. Stop it in a way that relates to the offense.

Following are examples of logical consequences.

- If a child breaks a toy, don't replace it.
- If a toddler bangs her spoon on her highchair, take it away.
- If a child leaves her bike out all night, don't allow her to ride it for three days.
- If a child hits another child on the playground, make him sit out for 5-10 minutes.
- If a child refuses to eat dinner, don't let him eat anything else until breakfast.
- If a child leaves clothes all over the floor, don't wash them until she puts them in the hamper.
- If a child's grades drop, take away his TV/video time until his grades improve.
- If a child forgets to do his homework, make him do his homework first before TV or play.
- If a child is using his cell phone inappropriately, replace it with a basic phone that does not text or have a data plan.

Consider the case of Sarah. When her son came home late one night, instead of getting mad, she sweetly said, "I'm so glad you're home safe. I was so worried about you. Next weekend you'll have to stay home so I won't have to worry." Or, one mother told her teenager, "Next time you go somewhere, I'm going to pick you up to make sure you come home on time." I even heard of one mother who told her teenager, "I lost so much sleep waiting up for you that I'll be too tired to do my chores tomorrow. You'll have to do them while I nap."

Time-out / Isolation

The whole idea behind time-out is when children break a known rule, they have to go to a designated area for a certain period of time. Often the children are told to think about their misbehavior and how they plan to behave correctly the next time.

If your child is a pre-toddler, time-out might be in a playpen or crib. For the post-toddler, time-out can be in a designated chair, the corner, a time-out mat (rug), or in his or her room. The important factor in where to have time-out is it should be away from anything fun and it shouldn't be too comfortable (such as a lounge chair).

Time-out is especially effective when your children are being cranky or obnoxious. Simply say something like, "You have a choice: You can either act nice, or you can go to your room for time-out. Which do you want to do?" Unless they perk up instantly, send them to their room until they have a more pleasant attitude.

The length of time children should stay in time-out will depend on the age of the children and their offense. A good rule of thumb is, if the offense is not great, one minute for every year of the child's age. For instance, if the child is three, time-out is for three minutes.

Increase the time for each offense of the same behavior. If Luke has to sit out for 5 minutes for throwing sand in his brother's face, make him sit out 10 - 15 minutes if he does it again. Just be reasonable with the time. You want time-out to be a deterrent, and yet you don't want to make it so long that it's unreasonable.

The best way to keep track of the time your children are in time-out is with a timer. I learned this lesson in a most unfortunate way my first year of teaching. I had a student misbehave during a spelling game, so I told him to sit in the hall. I planned to have him come back when the game was over; however, as they say, out of sight, out of mind. About an hour later, as we were leaving for recess, I realized he was still out there. From that time since, I have never put a child in time-out without setting the timer. It's just too easy to forget.

What if you can't get your children to stay in time-out? That means you don't have control over them yet, and you better get it now. Today, you can't get them to stay in time-out. Tomorrow, you can't get them to come home at night.

Solve the problem with a training session. At a neutral time, teach your child exactly how you expect them to behave in time out. And be sure to let them know that the consequence they'll receive for not staying in timeout will be far worse than the original time-out. Outright disobedience is not a trivial matter.

Loss of Privileges

To make losing a privilege effective, take away a privilege your children absolutely love and will upset them greatly if they don't have it. For instance, if your daughter only occasionally uses her iPad, that's not a good privilege to take away. However, if she's glued to her cell phone and it would devastate her to lose it, that's the privilege to take. (Note: You obviously shouldn't take away a young child's blankie or teddy bear. Loss of privilege is best for post-toddlers.)

As with any consequence, planning ahead will give you confidence and composure when the misconduct occurs. Make a list of the most important things or activities in your children's life. It might be watching TV, playing video games, being with friends, playing on the computer, driving the car, or going to a party. When misbehavior occurs, take away the privilege your child cherishes the most. Then, keep an eye on them to make sure the consequence is fully carried out. It does no good to take away TV privileges and then not notice as they quietly watch TV in another room.

If you work, and you just can't keep an eye on what they're doing at home, here are some ideas: if possible, take whatever privilege they've lost, somewhere else. Take their gaming system to a neighbor's, or put it in the trunk of your car. Or, you could put a parental control on your TV where only you know the passcode. Or, reset the password on your Wi-Fi. With all the technology available, there are ways to make sure your kids can't access a lost privilege.

If your children complain about the loss of privilege not being fair, remind them that it was a privilege that you took away, not a need. Tell them you will gladly supply the needs necessary for their survival, but privileges are only for those who obey the rules.

Grounding

Generally, grounding means children cannot leave their room or house except for school or activities for a certain period of time. There are many adaptations of grounding. Which one you choose will depend on the severity of the misdeed.

Some variations of grounding include:

1. Child is not allowed to leave the house except to go to school or parent-approved activities. No friends are allowed over during this period.
2. Child is not allowed to leave the house, plus he or she cannot watch TV, play video games, access the internet, etc.
3. Child is not allowed to leave his or her room for a certain period of time. All fun things are removed from his or her

room.

4. Child is not allowed to go anywhere or do anything fun until he/she accomplishes a certain number of deep cleaning household chores, such as cleaning out hall closet, cleaning out the garage, dusting all baseboards, vacuuming the car, etc.

5. Child is not allowed to go anywhere or do anything fun until they have earned 100 points. (Parent then makes a document showing ways to earn points, such as:

   - 10 points for memorizing 1 Bible verse about obeying parents.
   - 10 points for writing a letter to grandma.
   - 50 points for preparing and cooking dinner.

Whatever form of grounding you choose, be sure your children know exactly what they can and cannot do during this time frame. Being vague just opens the door for manipulation. And don't be hasty when deciding the grounding sentence. Calm down and include your spouse in the decision. Realize you will have to enforce whatever you decide. So be realistic. Grounding for a month is a long time in the life of a child. However, think in context of the violation. If your teen stays out all night, that definitely calls for a longer sentence. Make sure to give a definite time period to the grounding, as opposed to an open-ended amount of time.

I heard of one couple who grounded their son, but took his siblings out for a family fun night of pizza and go-cart racing. And they left the grounded child at home—with a very unpleasant baby-sitter.

Behavior Contracts

A behavior contract is a written agreement between parent and child that clearly states expectations, consequences, and sometimes privileges or rewards. These contracts are often made to stop an undesirable behavior, such as disrespect or a bad attitude. But many parents make contracts for allowances, chores, or cell phone use just so their children are clear about expectations.

Behavior contracts are usually used with teenagers and preteens. These contracts are useful for:

- Allowance

- Chores
- Pet Care
- Computer Use
- Cell Phone Use
- Technology Use
- Social Media
- Homework
- General Obedience
- Attitude and Respect
- School Behavior
- Drug, Alcohol, & Tobacco Use

While there can be many variations of a behavior contract, most include 3 parts:

1. Behavior expectations.
2. Consequence(s) for not meeting expectations.
3. Privileges or rewards for meeting expectations.

Three to ten behavior-related expectations are usually on a contract. Sometimes there is only one consequence or reward, and sometimes there are progressive consequences or rewards.

For instance, when my son, Hunter, was 13, he was frequently rude and disrespectful to me. My husband drew up a contract. Hunter had 3 expectations:

1. I will speak respectfully to my parents.
2. I will have a good attitude when I'm with my parents.
3. I will not argue with my parents.

His consequence for failing to abide by these rules was that he would be grounded for one week. If he did it again, he would be grounded for two weeks, and it progressed from there.

However, if he could go an entire week without being disrespectful, he got a snow cone. For two weeks of a good attitude, he got a snow cone and one golf club. For three weeks, he got one snow cone, another golf club, and a ticket to the water park. For four weeks, he got a snow cone, another golf club, another ticket to the water park, and a nice shirt from the mall. If he could go the entire six weeks without a disrespectful attitude, he got the rest of the set of golf clubs he wanted.

The downside, however, was that if he was disrespectful once, he had to start all over with the promised rewards. I recall that he messed up royally on the third week and had to start all over with just one snow cone!

There are lots of pre-written contracts on the internet. Or, you can look at the following sample contracts to create your own.

Teen Behavior Contract

1. I will have a respectful attitude toward my parents.
    a. Consequence: Grounded* for 1 week. Punishment doubles for each subsequent offense.
    b. Privilege: Use of car and access to friends and activities.
2. I will come straight home after school, unless I have permission from parent.
    a. Consequence: Will not be allowed to go anywhere after school for one week. Punishment doubles for each subsequent offense.
    b. Privilege: Will be allowed to go to after-school activities with permission of parent.
3. I will be home by 8 pm on school nights and 11 pm on non-school nights, unless I have permission from parent.
    a. Consequence: Grounded* for 1 week. Punishment doubles for each subsequent offense.
    b. Privilege: Will be allowed to stay out until curfew with parent permission.
4. I will do all assigned chores with a good attitude.
    a. Consequence: No TV, internet, cell phone, gaming, friends, or going anywhere until chores are completed.
    b. Privilege: May have access to technology, friends, and going places.
5. I will not use any alcohol, drugs, or tobacco.
    a. Consequence: Grounded* for 2 weeks. Punishment doubles for each subsequent offense.
    b. Privilege: Use of car and access to friends and activities.

Grounding consists of:
- No leaving the house except for school or parent-approved activities.
- No hanging out with friends.
- No TV, video gaming, or internet use.

_____ _____ _____ _____
Teen Signature   Date   Parent Signature   Date

Cell Phone Contract

1. I will always answer the phone when my parents call. I will keep my phone close so I do not miss their call.
2. I will text back immediately when I receive a text from my parents.
3. I will not use my cell phone after ____pm on a school night, and ____pm on a non-school night. I will keep my phone in my parents' bedroom during the night.
4. I understand that my parents have the right to read my text or go through my phone without my permission.
5. I will not text, take pictures, or video anything my parents would deem inappropriate.
6. I will not go over my monthly data plan; and if I do, I will pay for all costs.
7. I will leave my phone in my room during family dinners.
8. I will stop looking at my phone during family time or when my parents ask me.
9. I will not enable or disable settings without permission from my parents.
10. I will keep my phone in my backpack at school unless it is an emergency.

If I violate any parts of this contract, my consequence will be:

Immediate removal of cell phone, to be replaced with a basic cell phone that does not text or have a data plan.

_____   _____
Teen Signature   Date

_____   _____
Parent Signature   Date

Extra Chores

Some parents choose to have their children do extra chores as a consequence. I know one mom who has a Job Jar. She fills it with scraps of paper that say things like:

- Clean the top of the refrigerator.
- Organize the junk drawer.
- Weed the flowerbeds.

When one of her kids disobeys or is disrespectful, she makes them draw a chore out of the Job Jar and do it.

Early Bedtime

An early bedtime as a consequence is good for children who are being cranky or have a bad attitude. You might say, "Maybe you're being so grouchy because you haven't been getting enough sleep. You better go to bed an hour early tonight so you won't be so cranky tomorrow."

Fines

For a minor infraction, such as being messy, you might consider making your children pay a fine. For instance, you could have a rule where every time your children leave their shoes by the front door, they have to pay you a quarter. Or you might charge a dime for every article of clothing they leave on the bathroom floor. Or, if they don't clean up their toys on time, take their toys and make them buy them back for a dime a piece.

I personally am not a big fan of fines. I tried them when my sons were in middle school and they didn't really work well. But you could certainly give them a try.

If you do use fines, make sure that you don't give your children extra money to make up for the money they lost. For a consequence to be effective, it must cause some sorrow and suffering.

Restitution

Restitution is a wonderful consequence for when children damage property. Basically, it means that your children have to pay for any property they damage. And if they don't have the money to pay for the harm they caused, they need to get a job and use their paycheck to reimburse the offended party. Not only is this the right thing to do, it allows children to see how hard one has to work in order to buy something.

When Hunter and Skyler were 12, we stayed at my brother-in-law's lake house. He had boats and a golf cart. On the last day of our visit, they were recklessly driving the golf cart and crashed it.

Of course, they didn't have the $800 to fix it, so my husband made them work it off. They had to go to my brother-in-law's ranch for an entire week and paint fences.

If the offended party wants restitution immediately, you as the parent might want to pay for it, and then make your child work to pay you back.

Letter of Apology

If a child has been especially disrespectful or hurtful to someone in the family, sometimes a letter of apology is an appropriate consequence. (Depending on the severity of the offense, the letter of apology might be in addition to another consequence.)

When Hunter was in sixth grade, he spit on his brother. We made him write a letter of apology. Since we told him it had to be an entire page long, he just started rambling off a long list of confessions. Here are some of the excerpts:

> *Dear Skyler,*
> *I am so sorry for spitting on you. I also annoy you, and go in your room and fart on your pillow. I turn on your amp, steal your money, and kick and punch you. I hide your things, throw pens at you, and hit you with my fist. I also spit on your guitar posters.*
> *I pledge from this day forward not to hit or spit on you for the rest of my days. I hope you will forgive me.*
> *Your Brother,*
> *Hunter*

Whatever Bothers the Child Most

When deciding which consequence to use, think of what will upset your child enough to stop the bad behavior.

I love the story by Dr. James Dobson in his book *The New Dare to Discipline* about when he was a teenager misbehaving in school. No amount of discipline seemed to change his bad attitude. So one day his mother told him if she ever received a call from his principal about his bad behavior she was going to school with him the next day. She was going to walk right behind him all day and hold his hand. She was going to enter into all his conversations with his friends. She was going to be by his side the entire day at high school. No punishment would have been worse for him. His attitude and grades immediately improved!

I know one couple who couldn't seem to find a consequence that worked with their daughter. (Time-out didn't bother her because she loved to read alone in her room, and they didn't want to take books away from her.) So instead, they made her move a pile of bricks in their back yard from one side to the other. She hated it, so that was the consequence they used with her. Do whatever bothers your child the most.

Spanking

Warning: This section may be politically incorrect!

I have thought long and hard about including the topic of spanking. Because in modern day America, spanking is considered sadistic and is equivalent to child abuse. So I personally, am not going to advocate spanking. Instead, I just want to share with you my humble experience and memories about the topic. Because parenting techniques have changed drastically in the last 30 plus years. What was once considered the right way to discipline, is now considered the wrong way. So let's start, with a brief history.

For the first 200 years of the United States, parenting methods were based on Biblical principles. Whether someone was a believer or not, Biblical principles were the norm. And the Bible taught that parents should have authority over their children, and that they were to use the rod to discipline.

But starting in the late 1940s, parenting techniques slowly began to change. Intellectual elites and child psychologists concluded that traditional, biblical parenting methods were not only incorrect, but were psychologically damaging. Among other things, these new parenting experts told parents that they should absolutely never spank.

It took about 30 years to get this kind of thinking into mainstream America. Because until about the 1980s, using the rod to discipline was still very much the norm.

For example, my parents and in-laws were born between 1925 and 1930. They have all assured me that most everyone in their generation was spanked. Yet they were known as …. The Greatest Generation. My mom said they never locked their doors at night, yet never worried for their safety. And this was during the Great Depression when poverty was rampant.

My husband and I were born in 1960 and 1961. When I was in grade school, every single teacher had a large wooden paddle on her desk. If a student misbehaved, the teacher would give the misbehaving student one or two swats in front of the class. It honestly didn't happen very often. Since we knew we would get spanked if we disobeyed, we were generally pretty good. And back then, there was a standard rule for most kids: If you got paddled at school, then your parents would spank you twice as much when you got home. (Parents didn't even think about suing the teachers back then! They were usually embarrassed their child had misbehaved.)

When I was in junior high and high school, teachers would send students who misbehaved to the principal's office for swats. When I was a senior in 1979, I worked in the school office. I remember how teachers would buzz the intercom to tell the principal she was sending a student. The principal would take the guilty student into his office. I could hear him say, "You are not allowed to act like that in Mrs. So-and-so's class. You are to be respectful and do what she tells you." Then, I would hear two or three swats. But again, it was very rare. Because the threat of swats was there, we really didn't have that much misconduct in class.

When I was growing up, every one of my friends and family were spanked. The thing about it, though, is we really weren't spanked very often at all. Most of us were rarely ever spanked after the preschool years. We knew our parents *would* spank us; therefore, we generally were pretty good.

Even on TV, spanking was promoted. One of the most popular shows when I was growing up was *The Andy Griffith Show*. There was one episode that I remembered that I recently found on YouTube. It was from 1963, and it was about a new boy who moved to Mayberry who was rude and disobedient. His father did nothing to discipline him. Finally in the end, however, Andy gave the father some of his common sense wisdom. The father ended up taking the boy out to the woodshed to be spanked. And that was the happy ending. Barney and Andy smiled, and the audience clapped because finally the father had done the right thing and spanked the unruly boy.

That's the way it was when I was growing up. What's my point? Most everyone age 50 or more was spanked when they were young. According to the internet and parenting "experts" that would mean that most people over

50 are either violent, depressed, child abusers, or in prison. Is that reality? Every single one of my friends were spanked, and they are some of the nicest, kindest people you'll ever meet. Notice I said spanked—not beaten. We got a couple of well-deserved swats on the bottom. That's it.

Now I do need to add a disclaimer. All the friends and relatives I'm speaking about came from good and loving families. As far as I know, none of the parents were drug users, alcoholics, or had anger issues. I'm sure it would be a different story for children who had parents like this.

So in 50 years, we've gone from spanking being considered a good thing, to spanking being considered a bad thing. And not spanking— which used to be considered a bad thing—is now considered a good thing.

Again, I am not advocating spanking. However, I'd like the younger generation to hear a different perspective than what you read on the internet.

10
THE EFFECT OF TV AND TECHNOLOGY ON A CHILD'S BRAIN DEVELOPMENT

Most parents are familiar with the many studies that link violence, aggression, obesity, and risky behaviors to watching too much television. But are you aware of the abundance of research that suggests watching too much television as a young child may actually alter a child's brain structure and cause future learning problems?

The evidence of negative effects on a child's brain is so great that The American Academy of Pediatrics (AAP) recommends absolutely no screen time for children under age two. (Screen time includes anything with a screen: TV, video games, smart phones, computers, tablets, etc.) Many pediatricians recommend no screen time for children under age three, while some go as far as no interactive screen time before the age of 10. (In 2008, France actually banned French channels from airing TV shows aimed at children under the age of three.)

For children age two to five, the AAP recommends no more than one hour of total screen time per day, co-viewed with a parent. For school-age children, ages 6 to 18, the AAP recommends no more than one to two total hours of screen time per day.

Now why would the American Academy of Pediatrics make these recommendations? What do they know that parents don't?

There's an abundance of research that suggests that watching too much television as a young child may actually change the anatomical structure of a child's brain and cause future learning problems. In the book, *Endangered Minds: Why Our Children Don't Think*, neuropsychologist Dr. Jane Healy explains how the way children spend their time in early childhood determine the neural wiring of their brain. And with so many children spending a large chunk of their day watching media, their brains are not developing properly.

Think about it. We are now experiencing a national crisis in academic learning, not only with "disadvantaged kids," but also with kids from every class. Students from elementary schools to universities are deficient in reading, writing, oral language, math, and science. According to The National Institute for Literacy 50% of U.S. adults can't read a book written at an eighth grade level; and 45 million are functionally illiterate and read below a 5th grade level. It's also interesting to note that the scores of the Scholastic Aptitude Test (SAT) began to drop at approximately the same time as the first TV generation—children who watched TV in their preschool years—began to take the test.

Also disturbing is the dramatic rise in learning disabilities, attention deficit disorders, and autism-spectrum disorders. Something is definitely going on. Could television and other media be the culprit?

In this chapter, I want to present the research about the effects of too much screen time on a child's development. All of the references for this information are at the end of the book. While I have tried to summarize and make the complex understandable, I highly encourage you to examine the research for yourself, and come to your own conclusion.

Neural Development

The first three years of a child's life are the most critical for brain development. In the first two years alone, a baby's brain actually triples in size.

A baby is born with about all the neurons (brain cells) his brain will ever need. A single neuron, however, has no power. The power of a neuron comes when it is connected to other neurons. In order to have a "good" brain for learning, the brain needs to have strong and widespread neural connections.

However, a baby is born with only about 17% of his neurons connected. The trillions of connections still to be made will be wired together in the years to follow. But it's the connections that form in early childhood that provide either a strong or weak foundation for the connections that form later.

These neural connections are made in two ways: genetics and most importantly, experience. It is the activities children experience during their first few years of life that determine how their brain is connected or wired. Today, however, a major source of experience for children is watching media.

How to Optimize Brain Development

There are two ways to develop a "good" brain for learning. A growing child needs both:

1. Lots of face-to-face human interaction
2. Play

Brains Grow with Lots of Human Interaction

Research has shown that the most important factor in increasing mental ability and making neural connections is for parents to talk frequently to their child. Caregivers need to sing, read, tell stories, and basically talk about everything that is going on. Neuropsychologist Alexander Luria asserts that language physically constructs the brain's higher-reasoning centers.

Many parents, however, mistakenly believe that TV will improve their child's language skills. In reality, it's just the opposite. Watching too much TV can actually delay a child's language development.

That's because television rarely allows the child to interact with it. Usually the pace is too fast, and the very nature of TV makes interaction unnecessary. Also, most children's programs are mainly visual, so there is really little need to listen.

With a real person, however, there's a back and forth interaction. The parent says something, and the child says something back. There's constant feedback and reinforcement. Plus, research shows that the language centers in a baby's brain grow with individualized, face-to-face interaction. It is conversation, not listening to media, that is the best way for children to develop language.

Children also need to practice talking. This practice talking helps to:

• Refine grammar

- Expand vocabulary
- Express ideas in an organized, coherent form
- Develop more complex abilities of thought
- Learn how to plan and to reason

This practice talking will eventually lead to inner speech. This inner speech will help them think through more complicated problems later in life. Many theories claim this lack of inner speech is what causes children to be impulsive and not think before they act. The theory goes that children who develop an inner speech will be able to think through problems first, before acting.

Television and other screen time, however, do not encourage children to talk. In fact, TV encourages the exact opposite. Instead of practicing their speech, children are passively watching the screen.

Add this to the fact that many children in their critical years for language acquisition are left in day-care centers all day, which often encourage the children not to talk. Overburdened or uninterested teachers often discourage interaction between the students or the teachers. Much of the day is spent either in teacher-directed large-group activities or watching TV.

In the pre-television era, small children would often follow their mother around the house as she did her usual household chores. As the mother would cook or clean, she would often talk out what she was doing. Now, however, if parents need to get something done, they often turn on the television. Children of today get very little "quality" conversations with adults.

Brains Grow with Play

The second way to develop strong and widespread neural connections is through play. Play is the natural way children learn. Play develops not only children's brains, but their physical coordination as well.

It is through play that children build the basic foundation for learning. Play develops:

- Mental skills such as problem solving and cause and effect
- Verbal skills
- Creativity and imagination

- Social skills
- Fine and gross motor skills

Through play children actively learn about the real world by investigating and experiencing it directly. They learn problem solving by interacting in their environment and figuring out how things work. They learn cause and effect by doing something and then seeing what happens.

I remember when Skyler was less than 18 months old. He would walk around the house and investigate everything. He would open and shut the door over and over. He was figuring out how the doorknob and latch worked. He would get on his stepstool and turn the faucet on and off. Then he would look under the sink to see where the pipes led. Today, Skyler is an engineer. He is so good at problem solving and fixing things! Every time he fixes something, I think about all the hours he spent investigating as a toddler. I'm so thankful I didn't plop him down in front of the TV. Instead, I made him play, and now his brain is wired to figure things out.

Researchers have found that brain connections in animals actually sprout during periods of play, and believe that the same kind of brain growth occurs in human children when they play.

Play also develops good verbal skills. When young children play, they frequently talk to themselves. They talk to their dolls, their stuffed animals, or just themselves. As stated before, practice talking hones their verbal development.

Play also develops children's imagination, creativity, and resourcefulness. When children play, they make up scenarios with their dolls or stuffed animals. They create things out of blocks or cushions. They invent toys out of sticks and boxes. Creativity and resourcefulness are important skills to develop for future endeavors.

How TV Hinders Brain Development

Watching excessive amounts of television does not promote widespread neural connections in children. Instead, it establishes strong, overbuilt connections for that specific skill area, but at the expense of developing connections in other areas of the brain. And, if neural pathways are not developed in other areas of the brain during the formative years, the potential neural foundations will be eliminated.

In other words, use it or lose it.

In addition, watching television may underdevelop higher-level thinking skills. The prefrontal lobe of the brain enables higher-level learning. Since mental effort develops the prefrontal lobe, and since television requires little mental effort, children who spend lots of time in front of the TV may not fully develop their prefrontal lobe. Consequently, as they get older and have the need for higher-order organizational abilities, they will realize that their brain doesn't "think" that way. The neural foundation was never built.

Watching excessive television in the early years doesn't mean that children won't learn to read words. Often these children do fine until about the fourth grade when higher-level skills are needed. But without full development of the prefrontal functions, it may mean they are unable to do more complicated forms of thinking such as comprehending well, analyzing, reasoning, assimilating, and using logic.

Not only does watching TV hinder their mental development, it impedes their physical development as well. At a time when young children should be practicing their physical coordination by running and climbing, and coloring and building, they're sitting immobile in front of the television.

Left and Right Brain Hemispheres

As you may recall, the brain is divided into two parts: the left hemisphere and the right hemisphere. Each hemisphere has a different function, yet they both work together. A good brain for learning will have strong connections between the two hemispheres. These connections can quickly and efficiently assign different aspects of a task to the most efficient part of the brain. Watching too much TV, however, causes both hemispheres to shrink and not make proper connections.

The left hemisphere is the academic and logical side of the brain. It manages:

- Spoken language
- Written language
- Math skills

- Science skills
- Reasoning
- Logic

The right hemisphere is the more creative and artistic side of the brain. It controls:

- Emotion
- Artistic awareness
- Musical awareness
- Spatial skills
- Imagination

The left hemisphere is processed through hearing, while the right hemisphere is processed through seeing. Television for young children is mainly visual, therefore it is processed primarily through the right hemisphere. Normally, both hemispheres process information together. But research has found that when we watch TV, right brain activity increases, while left brain activity decreases. The conclusion is that watching TV neglects the development of the left hemisphere. Reading, writing, spelling, math, science, and logic rely mainly on the left hemisphere.

Not only do strong connections between the two hemispheres improve a child's intellectual skills, but these strong connections will improve a child's physical, emotional, and social development as well.

Focused Verses Reactive Attention

Have you ever wondered why your child can pay attention to a screen for hours on end, yet seems to have no attention span for learning?

According to Dr. David Walsh in his book *Smart Parenting, Smarter Kids: The One Brain Book You Need to Help Your Child Grow Brighter, Healthier, and Happier*, the brain is equipped with two types of attention systems: reactive and focused. Reactive attention is instinctive, automatic, and involuntary. It is located in the emotional part of the brain and is naturally drawn to movement and sound. This natural instinct is needed for danger.

Focused attention, however, must be developed with practice.

Focused attention is located in the prefrontal cortex—where higher learning takes place. Focused attention is needed to learn.

Dr. Walsh contends that screen time mainly involves reactive attention. Focused attention, however, is developed through play and human interaction.

Background TV

Background TV is television that a child can see and hear, but is not actively watching. Researchers have found that even if a child is not watching the TV, it can still delay a young child's language. How? When the TV is off, a caregiver will speak an average of 940 words per hour if a toddler is around. However, if the TV is on in the background, the caregiver only speaks about 170 words per hour! Remember, the main way to increase mental ability is for the parent to talk frequently to their child. The less a parent talks, the less their child develops mental ability.

Also, research has found that when the TV is on in the background, children were less likely to focus on their hands-on play.

Too Much TV or Too Little Time in Natural Learning Activities?

So, are these brain alterations caused directly by watching TV? Or, are the changes in the neural wiring due to all the time taken away from playing and interacting with adults?

Children's brains are designed to learn from face-to-face interaction and play. But consider this: The typical preschooler watches an average of four to five hours of television each day—that's about 40% of the time they're awake! That's 40% of their waking hours taken away from developing and honing their fundamental competency skills.

Recent studies found that school-age kids spend an average of seven-and-a-half to nine hours a day in front of either a television, a computer, a smartphone, or another digital device. That's seven-and-a-half to nine hours a day they could have spent reading, being physically active, doing homework, developing social skills with friends, and interacting and learning values from family.

Whether the alterations in a child's brain structure is caused by viewing TV or time taken away from doing healthy activities is unclear. But either way, is watching TV and other media worth the risk?

Learning Disabilities

Since 1955, the number of learning disabilities has grown steadily. Is it mere coincidence that television became a standard household fixture around that time?

Psychologist and author John Rosemond in his book, *Six-Point Plan For Raising Happy, Healthy Children,* believes that watching too much television in the formative years is responsible for not only the downward shift of scholastic achievement tests, but also for the steady increase in learning disabilities. In his book, he notes that the symptoms of a learning disabled child and the developmental skills that watching television fails to exercise are almost the same. Learning-disabled children have problems with:

- Listening
- Language
- Gross and fine motor skills (physical coordination)
- Problem solving
- Persistence
- Attention span

In other words, television takes a great deal of time away from the development of these fundamental competency skills.

Watching excessive amounts of television inhibits the development of all the above skills. Learning-disabled children have problems with:

Listening: Since most children's programs are mainly visual, active listening is not really required to understand what is going on. Some researchers believe that one reason children haven't built those important auditory processing connections in their brains is because they have never really had to listen.

Language: As previously discussed, TV does not promote language skills. Passive listening requires no interaction and takes away time that children would have spent practicing their speech to themselves or with a caregiver.

Physical Coordination: Instead of running, jumping, skipping, coloring, building with blocks, cutting and pasting, and putting together puzzles, children often spend the majority of their waking hours sitting passively in front of the TV. Watching an inordinate amount of television does not develop fine or gross motor skills.

Problem Solving: Children develop problem solving abilities by playing. When children play, they come across many obstacles which they have to figure out. Through exploration and investigation, children learn problem solving techniques. Watching television does not encourage the diligence or effort needed to solve problems.

Persistence: Persistence is needed for almost every skill in school (and life). But watching too much TV seems to reduce a child's persistence with problems. With TV, everything is fast-paced, with little time to be bored. If it's boring, change the channel. But in real life, kids need the skill of being persistent in solving a problem.

With play, it takes time and persistence to figure out how to make things work. I remember Skyler spending hours building complicated structures with his assorted building sets.

Today, being persistent definitely describes Skyler. As an adult, he has accomplished so many difficult achievements. While yes he is intelligent, he accomplished most of them through sheer persistence and determination.

Attention Span: Many experts are now concluding television is causing shortened attention span in our nation's youths. Because the scene or camera angle changes every few seconds, viewers are never required to pay attention for more than a few seconds at a time. Some researchers fear that children's brains will get used to this overstimulation and wire the brain in ways that lead to a short attention span, which can affect learning.

Check out this phenomenon yourself. Turn on almost any children's program. Watch how often the scene or camera angle changes. It usually changes every three to seven seconds. In fact, most children's programs of today are incredibly fast-paced.

Compare that to an episode of *Mister Rogers' Neighborhood*, a children's television show that aired from 1963 to 2001. (You can see old episodes on YouTube.) It is painfully slow! Contrast that with almost any children's program of today. The difference in pacing is obvious.

Is television the reason for this outbreak in learning disabilities? While the evidence is not yet conclusive, the correlations are definitely note-worthy.

Attention Deficit Disorders (ADHD)

Across the country, growing numbers of children are being diagnosed with attention deficit disorder. (There's been a 50% increase just in the past 10 years!) Most cases, however, do not have any proven physical dysfunction of the central nervous systems. It leads us to question if possibly the environment or the way a child is raised is responsible.

It's interesting to note that many children with ADHD exhibit the same symptoms of learning disabled children. Some symptoms of children with ADHD are:

- Failure to listen
- Failure to persist
- Short attention span
- Acting before thinking (impulsive)

As discussed earlier, listening, persistence and attention span are skills that TV does not develop. Some researchers believe that television also encourages impulsive behavior, such as acting without thinking. Because television does not strengthen language development, many children never learn to think to themselves. When they fail to talk through problems in their own heads, they just act without thinking.

One theory that links TV with ADHD is that many programs, including *Sesame Street*, show sudden close-ups and zooms with quick movements, bright colors, and sudden noises. This attention-getting gimmick capitalizes on the brain's instinctive response to danger. As the picture zooms in quickly at the viewer, the viewer's brain prepares the body to respond, but then no physical action is taken. Researchers suggest that children, thus stimulated, without natural physical outlets for the stored-up response, might develop hyperactivity, frustration, or irritability. Other researchers have noted that children who watched excessive TV as a preschooler have neural wiring that looks like those who have ADHD.

Family psychologist John Rosemond raises the possibility that in certain cases, (perhaps most!), ADHD could be reversed if television were eliminated from the child's environment before the damage "sets." Neuropsychologist Dr. Jane Healy has noted many parents of children with ADHD who saw definite improvement after they took away television viewing privileges.

Autism

The number of children diagnosed with autism-spectrum disorders (ASD) has skyrocketed. According to the Centers for Disease Control and Prevention (2014), an estimate one in 68 American children have ASD. That's a 119.4 percent increase from 2000! A 2015 government survey of parents, however, suggests an even higher number—one in 45. Compare that with one in 2500 children 30 years ago.

Could there be a link between autism-spectrum disorders and the ever increasing numbers of infants and toddlers who watch TV? The average age a child watched TV regularly in 1970 was four years old. Today, the average age a child watches TV is four months! And the typical preschooler is watching about four-and-a-half hours of TV a day. That's about 40% of their day!

While the science is certainly not settled, there are studies that connect watching television as an infant or toddler to autism-spectrum disorders. (Vaccinations as a cause have been ruled out by most.) According to a 2008 research study, one in 300 children had autism. However, if they watched TV as a toddler, that number was one in 175. Other researchers found that autism rates began to rise dramatically at the same time cable television was introduced. They also noted that autism rates were higher in rainier parts of the country, suggesting that kids who stayed indoors more watched more TV.

The fact is, in today's culture, both parents and children are glued to some form of media for a large chunk of their day. And the more immersed in media family members are, the less they talk and socially interact. The less social interaction, the less the brain develops. Have you ever seen the famous brain scan of the child in the Romanian orphanage who was horribly neglected? His brain didn't develop.

Researchers have found that with less talk, children's brains are not wiring for communication skills, empathetic listening, and the ability to interpret and respond to nonverbal cues. Those are all symptoms of autism.

None of this proves television causes autism-spectrum disorders. However, with the many studies that assert TV changes a child's brain structure for the worse, it is a very compelling link. Why take the risk with your precious child?

Educational TV

Would it surprise you to know that many researchers are now concluding that educational TV for young children does more harm than good? The American Academy of Pediatrics (AAP) asserts that there is no such thing as educational TV for children under two. They believe that not only is TV not educational for babies and toddlers, it could actually hinder their development.

First of all, *Sesame Street* is not a prerequisite to learning to read. In fact, the literacy rate in this country was far higher before *Sesame Street* was introduced. Yes, *Sesame Street* is good at teaching letter and number recognition. But at what price? Does watching *Sesame Street* make strong and widespread neural connections in a developing brain?

Studies indicate that children who were permitted to watch many hours of television in their preschool years scored lower on reading, math, and language tests compared to children who had watched little TV during their preschool years. In fact, research clearly shows that students who tend to watch less TV do better in school than those who watch more TV.

The long-term effect of watching so much television is far more damaging then the superficial benefit of being able to spout off the alphabet and count to 20. As discussed earlier, watching excessive television in the formative years can hinder the development of the basic competency skills needed to succeed in school. Watching television does not promote language, listening, problem solving, persistence, and especially attention span. Developing these basic skills are the true building blocks of intellect.

Pre-academic skills such as those learned on *Sesame Street*, can be learned quickly and easily just by reading alphabet books and counting in everyday, ordinary conversations.

In addition, children who learn from education shows come to school wanting to be entertained. If the poor teacher doesn't have a dancing alphabet, she's likely to lose their attention.

It is much more important to lay the basic foundation of learning in the preschool years than it is to put trivial bits of information into their minds via the TV. And the way to lay that foundation is through human interaction and play.

Television and Technology for Infants and Toddlers

Television, videos, and technology directed at infants is a relatively new phenomenon. Ten to fifteen years ago, there was very little infant TV viewing. But in the late 1990's, *Baby Einstein* came out. Since then, videos and technology marketed to infants have exploded. Today, almost all American infants and toddlers are exposed to TV or videos for about one to two hours a day. If you include background television, infants and toddlers are exposed to television for an average of four hours each day.

Here's the problem: Infants watching TV is so new that no one really knows if it's safe or not. The research so far, however, suggests that it is NOT safe for infants and toddlers to watch television.

Pediatrician and researcher Dr. Dimitri Christakis is concerned that Americans are overstimulating their infants developing brains. His research shows that all this fast-paced media is having a negative effect on young children's growing brains. He states that watching TV before the age of 18 months has lasting negative effects on children's:

- Language development
- Reading skills
- Short-term memory
- Attention span

Infant and toddler television exposure also contributes to sleep problems, and TV viewing at age three has been linked to behavior problems and long-term effects on social development.

Babies and toddlers are not designed to learn from watching TV. As stated earlier, infants and toddlers learn in two ways:

1. Lots and lots of face-to-face human interaction
2. Hands-on play and exploration in the real world

Again, babies and toddlers needs lots and lots of conversation. They need back and forth social interaction. Caregivers need to sing, read, rhyme, count, and talk about everyday situations.

Babies also need a safe place to explore the real world. Babies don't know anything about textures, shapes, smells, shadows, and weights. You can't learn that from a two-dimensional TV screen! They need three-dimensional hands-on exploration to learn about their physical world around them. And when babies reach for, rattle, and throw their toys around, they're developing hand-eye coordination.

Many parents allow their baby to watch TV because it looks as if the baby enjoys it. Babies and toddlers are mesmerized by these videos. The brain's natural instinct is to be drawn to motion and bright colors. But just because a baby stares at the screen doesn't mean his brain can process the images he sees.

There's frankly not enough evidence to show that these products directed to infants are safe. Yet there's convincing evidence to suggest they are not. Why risk it?

The Negative Effect of Screen Time on Sleep

If your children have a hard time going to sleep, staying asleep, and waking up refreshed, the problem could be screen time. Watching an electronic screen an hour before bedtime or naps arouses your brain, not winds it down.

Normally, as it gets dark, your body starts to secrete a hormone called melatonin, which helps you sleep. But the blue light emitted from screens makes your body think it's still daytime. This light prevents the body from releasing the sleep-inducing hormone melatonin. On the opposite side, exciting video games, scary movies, or stimulating TV shows can release a hormone called adrenaline— which keeps you alert.

Add the fact that children are staying up later to engage in media, and you've got a nation of sleep-deprived kids. This chronic sleep loss contributes to all kinds of health issues such as:

- Behavior problems and aggression
- Depression
- Weight gain
- Stress

- Lack of energy and alertness
- Weakened immunity

Children need lots of sleep to develop both mentally and physically. That's why the American Academy of Pediatrics, among others, recommend no screen time at least an hour before bedtime and naps. So have your kids look at a book to wind down, not a screen.

Video Game and Screen Addiction

There's a new and very real problem immerging in the United States—video game and screen addiction. According to one study, one in 12 gamers become addicted.

In his book *Glow Kids: How Screen Addiction is Hijacking our Kids--and How to Break the Trance*, Dr. Nicholas Kardaras contends that young children exposed to too much screen time are at risk of developing an addiction "harder to kick than drugs." He calls it "digital heroin." Kardaras points to brain-imaging research that confirms glowing screens affect the brain's frontal cortex in precisely the same way that drugs like cocaine and heroin do.

One research study done by the United States Military on combat burn victims found that playing video games was just as an effective pain killer as morphine!

The question is: What effect is this digital drug having on the brains and nervous systems of young children? Are we naively allowing a future addiction to take hold of our children?

Technology and School-age Children

While the brain's main growth spurt is in the preschool years, the brain continues to develop until about the age of 25. During the teen years, the prefrontal cortex is being developed, which is responsible for problem solving, processing complex thoughts, and causing emotions. A 2010 study showed the average teenager spends more than seven hours a day staring at a television, computer, or smart phone. A 2015 survey, however, found that teens are spending an average of nine hours a day using media! Check out the problems associated with teens spending too much time on media:

- Weight gain
- Sleep deprivation
- Lack of exercise
- Interference with family time, which is the time you pass on your morals and values
- Weakened social skills
- Chronic distraction
- Little time to read and do homework
- More aggressive
- Less sympathetic
- More apt to engage in sexual behavior

Most of the above problems could be averted just by following the one to two hours media limit recommended by the American Academy of Pediatrics.

Fear of Being Technologically Left Behind

Many parents reason they must introduce technology early or their children will be left behind. But today's interfaces are so user-friendly, most kids can figure them out quickly. It can be likened to driving a car. You want your children to know how to drive by age 16. Does that mean you should allow them to practice as young children? No! They'll pick it up quickly when they need the skill.

Screen Time Recommendations

How much screen time a child should be exposed to varies from expert to expert. Some recommend no screen time until 18 months old, while others advocate waiting until age three. One leading expert argues for no interactive screen time until age 10! Here's a summary of the recommendations:

From The American Academy of Pediatrics:

- Age 0-18 months: Zero screen time with the exception of video chatting to family members.

Age 18-24 months: Media can be introduced *if* it is co-viewed with a parent. That means it's okay *if* a parent is sitting there talking about what is happening on the screen. It is not recommended that children age 18 to 24 months watch media alone.

- Age 2-5: No more than one hour of high-quality programming a day, preferably co-viewed with a caregiver.
- Age 6-18: One to two *total* hours of digital media a day. (Computer time for homework is separate and not included in the two-hour limit.)
- No TV on in the background for preschoolers.

Author and psychologist John Rosemond recommends that children shouldn't be allowed to watch any television until they have learned to read and have learned to read well. After that, he recommends you only allow your child to watch five hours a week.

Author and psychotherapist Dr. Nicholas Kardaras believes that kids below the age of 10 should have no use of video games or interactive screens (tablets or smart phones). He asserts excessive screen time leads to clinical disorders.

While experts may disagree on how much, they do agree on this: absolutely no TV, video games, computers, or any type of electronics in the bedroom!

Here's a condensed list of Do's and Don'ts from the leading authorities:

Do's

1. Have family rules limiting media use and enforce them.
2. Have a technology curfew—at least one hour before bedtime—where no screen usage is allowed.
3. Have children charge or leave all smart phones, tablets, etc., in parent's bedroom at the established curfew.
4. Place family computer in a public spot in the house (such as the kitchen) so parents can monitor computer use.
5. Have parental controls with both ratings and time limit on all media devices. (Some parental controls are built-in

and can be accessed in "Settings." However, you may need to invest in technology that adds parental controls.)

6. Set rules about new technology before it is introduced.
7. Talk to your children in the car or restaurants instead of automatically letting them watch media.
8. Pay attention to all media in which your children are involved, including games and apps.
9. Spend time with your kids teaching proper online etiquette, including topics such as giving out personal information, inappropriate pictures or language, cyberbullying, and sexting.
10. Understand and follow media ratings for TV, video games, and movies.
11. Make it clear to your children that you will be checking all of their internet activity daily, and that includes all of their social media. Get their passwords for all social media accounts.
12. If texting is allowed, make it clear to your kids that you have the right to read their texts at any time. If anything is deemed inappropriate, their texting plan will be cut.
13. Check all browsing history on the internet daily, and don't allow them to delete browsing history.
14. Avoid fast-paced media—especially for young children.
15. Establish rules where TV is only allowed after all homework and chores are completed.
16. Consider having a weekday ban on all technology, and let TV be a weekend treat.
17. Let your child's other caregivers know about your media rules.
18. Set a good example with your own media use.

Don'ts

1. Don't allow TVs, video games, computers, tablets, or any electronic media in your child's bedroom—even when they are teenagers.

2. Don't have the TV on in the background if you have preschoolers.
3. Don't allow any type of screen time during family meals.
4. Don't allow your child to be involved in any media that doesn't have parental controls set up.
5. Don't allow screen time one hour before bedtime.
6. Don't allow children to watch inappropriate media.
7. Don't use TV as a discipline tool or as a way to calm your children down. Teach them to behave properly without having to pacify them with media.
8. Don't allow virtual reality headsets for children under 13. (Actually, we still don't know the health risks of these headsets at any age.)

11
THE IMPORTANCE OF PLAY

So what in the world are your children going to do if they don't watch TV or play video games? The answer is: Learn to play independently and entertain themselves!

Being able to play independently and entertain themselves is so important to the development of children. As discussed in Chapter 10, play is the natural way children learn. Play develops:

- Strong and widespread neural connections in a growing brain
- Mental skills such as problem solving and cause and effect
- Verbal skills
- Creativity and imagination
- Social skills
- Physical coordination

Children also need to learn the skill of entertaining themselves. Without this self-direction ability, kids don't know what to do with themselves. If there's not specifically something for them to do, they get bored. And when children don't know how to occupy themselves productively, it leads to trouble. According to researcher and writer Alan Caruba, as kids get older and are unable to entertain themselves, they look to other things to amuse themselves like drugs, alcohol, and sex.

Therefore, independent, unstructured play—where children learn to entertain themselves—should be part of your children's daily routine. Instead of letting your children turn on the TV, tell them to play!

Independent Play

Independent play is simply when your children play alone or with siblings or friends, but without adult intervention. While you do need to spend time with your children playing and reading to them, this is not that time. During independent playtime, kids need to learn how to entertain themselves. (This does not include playing any type of video games or technology.)

Each day, have your children play independently *at least* an hour or two. This play can be in their room, outside, or somewhere away from you. Just make sure it's totally childproof.

For babies and toddlers, this independent play can also be in the same room with the parent. Just go about your business while your young children play near you.

When Skyler was little, he would follow me from room to room and play. If I was in the kitchen, he would bring his toys in the kitchen and play. When I went upstairs, he would bring his toy upstairs and play near me.

Teach Them to Play

In the beginning, you may need to spend some time teaching your children how to play and entertain themselves. For instance, teach your children how to give a tea party to stuffed animals. Or, demonstrate how to put a blanket over a card table to make a tent. Here are just a few ideas of things to teach your children to do during independent play:

- Color
- Paint
- Cut and paste
- Glue and glitter
- Make paper airplanes (There are lots of books at the library on paper airplanes.)
- Build model cars or airplanes
- String beads for necklaces

For developing the imagination, have lots of costumes on hand. Garage sales and thrift stores are great places to shop to stock the pretend center. My boys could spend hours playing and pretending in their costumes!

Toys

When buying toys, look for toys where children have to put forth creative effort and use their imagination. (Often simple toys are the best.) Limit toys that stifle the imagination like electronic toys where the toy does everything, and essentially the children just watch it instead of playing with it.

Here are some examples of toys that require thought and effort from your children: Building blocks and sets, Tinker Toys, Legos, Lincoln Logs, K'nex, dolls, Play-Doh, bats and balls, jigsaw puzzles, manipulative puzzles, coloring books, crayons, musical toys, board games, jump rope, Etch A Sketch, train set, kitchen set with plastic dishes, play tools, farm set with animals, beads and strings, etc.

A word of caution: In the beginning, it's likely your children won't want to play by themselves. But remember, think long-term. Children need to learn how to play independently in order to develop their basic competency skills.

When my twins were toddlers (I think about 18 months old) I added independent outside play to their routine. Every day I made them play in my fenced-in backyard. While Skyler adjusted to it quickly, Hunter did not want to go outside! He wanted to stay inside with me. So after I made him go outside, he would stand at the door and cry pitifully. While I didn't like to hear him cry, I knew he needed to play outside. So initially, I told him he had to stay outside until the timer rang—10 minutes. The first two days, he cried the entire time. A couple of days later, I would make him stay out 15 minutes and I increased it five minutes every couple of days. Within, a week he would cry for about a minute, and then realize that I wasn't letting him in. Then, he would turn around and start having fun. After a brief crying spell, I would see him running, climbing, digging, laughing, and having a great time. I was so glad I didn't give in.

After my sons learned how to play outside, they generally played outside most of the day. I admit, my backyard was fun. I had a swing set, a sandbox, a wading pool, and a playhouse. As they got older, they had bikes, roller blades, skateboards, etc. There was plenty to do outside.

So don't be afraid to make your children temporarily unhappy if you're doing what's best for them. Making them turn off the TV and play will take effort and firmness on your part. But in the long run, you will have produced children who can entertain themselves, leaving you with more time to get things done.

12
RESPONSIBLE DIGITAL PARENTING

How to Limit Television, Video Games, and Other Media

Before you try to curtail your family's viewing habits, explain to your children why you're doing it. Let them know that too much screen time could affect their mental and physical development, academic success, social skills, and their ability to entertain themselves. If they know you're doing this with their best interest in mind, it will be more bearable.

Next, set definite time limits, such as only one hour a day. It might be helpful to set the timer to ring at the end of their time limit to remind them to turn off the TV or device. Or, you could make it simple and make the rule of No-Screen Time on weekdays and only on weekends. If you can't possibly commit to that, consider having two days a week of No-Screen Time, and pronounce those days to be family days.

One of the easiest ways to set time limits on media is to buy a technology timer. These time management and parental control tools will work on the TV, video games, and the computer. Products like BOB is a TV and video game timer. When the child's time is up, the device automatically shuts down. Parents can override the timer with a master PIN. We used one of these devices when our boys were teenagers and it was great because we didn't have to nag them. They knew they had one hour a day and that was it. They had better use their media time wisely.

For mobile devices like a smart phone, tablet, or laptop, enforce a technology curfew. At least one hour before bedtime, have your children leave or charge all mobile devices in the parent's bedroom. Otherwise, you'll have no idea how late they stay up or what they're doing. (Not to mention how screen time at bedtime is associated with insufficient and poor quality of sleep.)

Finally, get your children on a structured routine. A structured routine makes sure you have high-priority activities—like reading, playing and chores—scheduled into their day. If your kids are following a good routine, there really won't be much time to watch TV. (Read the next chapter to find out what to include in your children's routine.)

Whatever rules are made concerning media use, with few exceptions, stand firm and consistent. That doesn't mean you can't be flexible. Just make sure your week is not characterized by giving in. Let babysitters or other caregivers know the rules concerning screen time too.

If you absolutely do find yourself needing to entertain your kids, consider getting audio books. (There are lots of audio books at the library that you can either check out or download free from home.) Listening to stories, as opposed to watching TV, will help develop their listening skills.

Of course, the best model of restraint is you the parent. Is the TV constantly on? How can you tell your children not to watch TV when you have it on every waking moment? If you must watch TV, try recording your favorite shows and watch them after the children are asleep.

How to Enforce Media Limits

It's hard to stick to a media rule when the children are begging, complaining, and making endless bargains to watch TV. How do you really enforce such a rule?

First of all, if you want your children to know you mean business, you must have conviction. Are you really convicted that watching too much screen time is harmful? If you're not convinced or if you think it really doesn't matter, that message will come across loud and clear to your kids. They'll know it will be worth the effort to keep bugging you. If, however, you truly believe TV and video games are harmful to the development of your children, you will enforce the rule. Think of it this way: Would you allow your child to play in a busy street? Of course not! You'd get serious and absolutely not allow it. If all depends on your convictions of certain things.

I first read how excessive TV could change a child's brain structure over 20 years ago. Because of that, I rarely allowed my boys to watch TV until third grade. (Even then, it wasn't often.) But my boys really didn't ask to watch TV very much. They knew I was serious about the No-TV rule. They knew unless they were throwing up or really sick that I probably wasn't going to let them.

I remember when I first started letting my sons watch TV, I made them run around the block three times for every 30 minutes they wanted to watch. I'd stand on the front porch and count their laps before I let them turn on the TV. They were so excited to finally get to watch TV, they didn't mind. (It's funny, they now both run 5Ks and often win in their category. Was running to watch TV the beginning of their race careers?)

Remember, the more you "give in" about watching television, the more your children will bug you about watching TV. If they feel like they've got a chance, they'll take the risk. However, when they know the answer is going to be a firm no, they won't even try.

If your family is already accustomed to watching excessive screen time, expect a withdrawal period. TV is addictive, and the first few weeks won't be easy. Kids who have never learned to entertain themselves will find themselves wandering around the house wondering what to do. Don't give up so easily. It takes time to learn how to play. But the many who do, as reported in Marie Winn's book *The Plug-In Drug*, end up saying it was the best thing they did for their family.

On a personal note, I think back through my 16 years of teaching and remember my absolute favorite student of all time, Ashley. Ashley had three siblings in school and they were everyone's favorite. Each year the teachers clambered to get one of these children in their class. They were a remarkable family. In fact, all four of them were probably the nicest, most well-behaved children I've ever met. But the thing I remember most about them is ... they had no TV.

Defiance of Media Rules

What if your children refuse to have their screen time limited? Then, it's a problem of obedience. Remember, house rules should not be subject to debate. Children can certainly have an input and you need to listen carefully and weigh their opinion. However, you as the parent have the final decision. Just let your children know that if they break the media limit rule, or if they grumble or complain about it, they will get a consequence. State the consequence from the beginning and then follow through completely.

Don't feel guilty when your children tell you, "Everybody else gets to!" My response to my boys was always, "Yes, but I want you to turn out better than everyone else." Just because other parents are making foolish decisions doesn't mean you should.

I admit, my husband and I did raise our sons more strictly than most parents. And it was hard when all their friends got to do things that they weren't allowed to do. But now, we're reaping the harvest of our diligent parenting. Our sons have turned out so well—hard working, well-mannered, responsible adults. I'm so glad I didn't allow them to do all the things their friends did!

Parental Controls

With all the inappropriate content in media, don't allow your children to get on any device that doesn't have strict parental controls set up. If you don't have the time or know-how to set up parental controls, then don't allow your children to have the device. Parental controls are an absolute must!

Beware though. No parental controls are foolproof. In fact, determined teens have a multitude of ways to bypass parental controls—and they pass this knowledge around. Clueless parents have no idea!

So do the research and check the reviews to get the absolute best parental control for your device. Some parents claim that since resourceful teens can bypass controls, using a router with a timer that denies access to the internet during certain periods of the day is the best. Whatever product you use, check your child's device often to make sure they haven't deleted or disabled the parental controls. (It's amazing how kids who don't know how to empty a dishwasher can easily dismantle parental controls!)

I love the story of the working mom who changed the Wi-Fi

password each day. In order to get the new password, her kids had to clean the kitchen. They then had to text her a picture of the clean kitchen. To make sure they weren't recycling old pictures, she required them to do something different each day, such as "Take a picture of a box of crackers on top of the stove." The next day they had to put a jar of pickles. Genius!

While no parental control is 100% reliable, here are some guidelines if you share a computer with your kids:

1. Give each family member their own separate user account.
2. Make sure your kids can't get on your account (administrative) so they can't change settings or install another browser that you don't know about.
3. Create a password to your account that your kids will never figure out.
4. Set your account so when your computer goes idle, it locks within minutes and requires a password. Otherwise, a teen could easily just continue on your account—with all the administrative settings!
5. Keep the computer in an open spot, such as the kitchen.

While parental controls are an absolute must, nothing beats good old-fashioned parental supervision!

Monitoring Texts, Internet Use, and Your Child's Location

Monitoring your children's texts, social media, location, and the websites they visit is a necessary part of being a responsible parent.

Remember, the prefrontal cortex of your child's brain is still developing throughout the teen years. According to Dr. David Walsh, this is the part of the brain that "helps us to think ahead, consider consequences, and manage emotional impulses and urges." In other words, this part of your teenager's brain is not fully developed yet! Therefore, their actions need to be supervised.

This rule of monitoring your children's texts and posts is not about invading privacy or lack of trust. It's about protecting our children. Making silly or foolish mistakes with texts and posts on the internet can have serious and lasting repercussions.

Frankly, teens don't have the wisdom or experience to be smart about media. For instance, do they understand that their texts and pictures can and probably will be passed around? (Very common with teens.) Do they understand that their best friend today might hate them tomorrow and want to embarrass them? Once you post it in writing or images, it's out there for all to see.

I knew of one couple who read their "trustworthy" 13-year-old's texts only to find she was texting with a 21-year-old man! Other parents discovered that their child was being bullied, or in an abusive relationship—all unknown to the parents.

By reading texts and posts, parents can find out what kind of friends their kids are hanging around. Often parents discover that their child's seemingly "good" friend is not a good influence after all.

The fact is, teens do stupid things—even the good kids—and the rules you set need to be checked. My motto throughout my sons' teen years was "Trust, but verify."

When my boys first got a Facebook account in ninth grade, I made it clear that I was going to check their profile page every day. (I had their passwords.) They knew if they ever posted any inappropriate language or content, I would immediately close their account. When your children know that you will be checking their digital communications, it will help keep them accountable for their actions.

If your child is truly trustworthy and not doing anything wrong, they shouldn't have a problem with you checking their texts. If they claim that it's too personal for their parent to read, then it shouldn't be sent out as a text—which can be passed around to others!

As your children near the end of high school, and prove trustworthy in other areas of life, it will be time to lighten up. Hopefully by then, they will understand the importance of what they put out on digital media.

Finally, a tracking app on your children's smartphones to verify their location is a great way to make sure your kids are where they're supposed to be. Letting your kids know that you will be checking their whereabouts will make them think twice before being deceptive.

13

GETTING YOUR CHILD INTO A STRUCTURED ROUTINE

If there's one thing I've learned as a teacher, it's that children function better in a structured routine. They love knowing what's going to happen each day. It makes children feel secure and confident.

I learned this lesson my first two years of teaching. In the beginning, I would change the order of our activities often so my students wouldn't get bored. I might do reading in the morning one day and then do it in the afternoon the next. I thought my students would enjoy the novelty. But things weren't going well. Finally, a seasoned teacher took me aside and told me how children need a structured routine. She explained that children love to do things at the same time each day so they know what's going on. It gives them a sense of control in their day.

She was so right! What a difference it made in my classroom. Just as children love to read the same story over and over again, children love the familiar. They love their days to be predictable. I soon discovered that when I strayed from the schedule, it upset some of the children. For instance, whether a child liked math or not, he would get upset if we didn't do it after storytime like we always did. And if elementary students need to be in a routine, how much more does a preschooler? (Even middle and high school students do better on some type of routine.)

Having your children in a structured routine doesn't mean that you have to do the exact same things each day. It simply means you follow the same pattern of activities each day at consistent times. For instance, mealtime, naptime and bedtime should be approximately the same time each day. Other activities such as playtime, family time and reading time might fit into some pattern as well. Although you can have a flexible time frame, the activities would follow a pattern.

Here is a sample preschooler's routine:

- Breakfast
- Read Aloud/ Storytime
- Independent Play
- Morning Snack
- Play (Inside or Outside)
- Lunch
- Nap
- Outside Play
- Snack
- Play or "Help" Make Dinner
- Dinner
- Family Time (Play or Read with Kids)
- Clean-up
- Bath & Brush Teeth
- Bedtime

With a routine, the child's day is predictable. You essentially follow the same pattern of activities each day.

What about shopping, visiting, or errands? No problem. This routine isn't etched in stone. Simply adjust the routine to meet your needs. However, try to stay within the pattern as much as possible. For instance, try to stick to a definite naptime and go shopping during their wake time. As long as most of the day is predictable, it's fine to throw in a few novelties.

If your children are in daycare, they're probably already on a structured routine. In other words, their snack, nap, lunch, and playtime is probably at the same time each day.

Schedule High-Priority Activities into Their Routine

To me, the most important reason to have children in a routine is to make sure high-priority activities are included each day. Imagine as a teacher if I didn't schedule in reading, writing, math, and science. If I didn't have a deliberate plan, I'd probably never get around to doing half of them each day. That's why it's so important to *schedule* important activities into your child's daily routine. Because as parents, it's so easy to go through the whole day (or week) and say, "Gee, I never read to my child today." Or, "Wow, the kids haven't played outside all week." With a routine, you make sure the important things are scheduled. Otherwise, your kids may end up watching TV or playing video games for way too many hours.

In fact, that's one of the cool parts about putting your children on a structured routine. If your kids are doing all the things they should be doing each day, they won't even have much time to watch TV. The problem of how to limit media will take care of itself.

In addition, if you present a routine as a way of life, it leaves little room for argument. For instance, if your children don't want to go to bed, say, "Sorry, but you know the rules. Seven-thirty is bedtime, and that's just the way it is."

Preschoolers and elementary-age children just function better if they adhere to a structured routine. A routine is also good for children diagnosed with Attention Deficit Hyperactivity Disorder (ADHD). It puts order into their otherwise frantic day.

Following are some high-priority activities you should consider putting into your children's daily routine:

- Good Morning Routine
- Snack
- Naps for Babies, Toddlers, and Preschoolers
- Read Aloud/ Storytime
- Independent Reading
- Independent Play
- Outside Play
- Homework
- Clean-up
- Bedtime

Good Morning Routine

Start the day out right. Get into the habit of being positive and loving when you wake up your children. It will set the tone for their day. Wake them up one minute early so you have time to cuddle, and tell them how much you love them.

Years ago I heard of "The Sixty-Second Rule." It was originally for spouses, but is great for your children too. The rule states that for the first sixty seconds in the morning—and the first sixty seconds when you see your child (or spouse) in the evening—you have to be totally positive. For sixty seconds you can't complain, be grouchy or negative. Instead, for sixty seconds you have to be loving, caring, and kind. After that, you can be your normal self. It really establishes the mood for the rest of the day.

Snack Routine

Get into the routine of giving your children a snack at approximately the same time each day. Children often get cranky and irritable simply because they're hungry. By establishing a scheduled mid-morning and mid-afternoon snack, parents can prevent the irritable hungries.

Read Aloud / Storytime

If you're not into a DAILY habit of reading to your kids, please add that to your routine. Children should be read to every day! Don't worry about teaching them how to read—just teach them to love to read.

Remember, talking frequently to your children is one of the best ways to promote brain development. Reading aloud literally strengthens your children's neural connections. It also improves your children's:

- Listening skills
- Attentiveness
- Vocabulary
- Background knowledge
- Imagination

And cuddling while reading a book provides a loving, bonding experience.

Make reading time fun. Get excited about books and show your children how much fun it is to read. Let your inhibitions go and really get into the characters of your books. When your children are babies or young toddlers, however, you might just want to point out objects in the pictures and name them.

It is never too early to start reading to your baby. The repetitions and patterns in nursery rhyme books are especially great for babies. I started reading to my twins when they were three months old. They loved it!

Make it a point to have lots of books in your house. For babies, get board or softcover books. If you can, make going to the library every week part of your routine. Most libraries will let you check out an unlimited amount of children's books. Plus, most libraries have all kinds of wonderful programs to get children excited about reading. Children's books are also easy to find at garage sales or thrift stores. So stock up and have plenty around.

Make sure your children's books are as accessible to them as their toys. Even babies love to "read" books by themselves. Before my babies could even walk, they loved to lie on their blanket and look at books. It kept them very entertained.

Don't think reading aloud to your children is over once they start school. Kids of all ages love to be read to. Read chapter books to them once your children hit second or third grade. I remember reading my boys the entire series of *The Boxcar Children*. They loved them!

How to Find Great Books

As a teacher, I've read thousands of children's books. I hate to say this, but there are a lot of really boring, dull books out there. However, there are also thousands of excellent books which will make your children excited to read. The question is: How do you as a parent know which books are both good and age-appropriate?

You could do it the old-school way. Take your kids to the library and have them find the books they want. The books might be good; they might not be. If you and your children enjoy that method, that's great. However, if you have no idea which books to get, here's a simple solution. Initially, it might take you some time to set up the accounts and figure this out. However, once it's all set up, it only takes moments to find great books.

1. Make an account on Goodreads.com. (Amazon also makes book lists, but I use Goodreads.)
2. Do an internet search for the best-rated or most popular books on Goodreads for your children's age. For instance, I might type in the browser "Goodreads + popular first grade books."
3. Click on a list and Goodreads will show you a long list of the best books for that age group. I always choose the best-rated books first that have thousands of reviews.
4. Now make an online account at your local library.
5. In the library search box, cut and paste a title of one of the great books listed on Goodreads.
6. When the book on the library search pops up, place a hold on that book.
7. Repeat the steps and place a hold on as many books as you want. (I used to check out 25 children's books a week when my boys were preschoolers. We read a lot!)
8. Wait for the email or text message telling you your books are ready for pickup.
9. Go to the library. Your books should be at the desk ready to check out.

I love this method for several reasons. First, you won't have to wander aimlessly around the library not knowing if a book is good or not. Plus, often the best books are already checked out. However, by ordering online, if your local library doesn't have the book, they'll order it from another library. Your chances of getting the great books you want are increased by ordering online.

Independent Reading

Once your children learn to read in first grade, add independent reading to your children's routine. It is so important that children read for at least 30 minutes per day.

One of the most essential skills your children need to learn is how to read well and at a good speed. Imagine going through middle school, high school, college, and then a job and not being able to read quickly and understand what you read. It would be pure torture. Assignments which should take 20 minutes to complete would take hours for a slow reader. Ack! Wouldn't it be kinder to enforce a little tough love and make sure they were good readers by 3rd grade?

So how exactly do you help your children become excellent readers? The answer is—add 30 minutes of independent reading to your child's daily routine. Because one of the key components to becoming an excellent reader is to practice, practice, practice!

Reading can be likened to playing tennis. As a child, I took tennis lessons. I know how to hold the racket, the proper way to swing, and how to keep score. But I'm a horrible player! Even though I *know* how to play, because I never practiced, I am really bad!

So it is with reading. Children can learn all the basic skills of reading, but if they don't practice, and practice often, reading will always be a struggle, which will only lead them to read less. Common sense tells you that the more children read, the better and faster they'll read.

So get your children into a DAILY habit of reading. I used to tell my first graders' parents to diligently practice reading with their children every night for 15-20 minutes until Christmas. After that, the majority of children should be able to practice on their own. They just need someone who makes them!

It would be lovely to think you could just encourage your children to read daily and they would. Sadly, that generally is not the case. Most children have to be forced to practice reading in the beginning—in a positive, encouraging way of course. Once they learn how to read quickly, however, you won't need to force them anymore. They will begin to read for pure pleasure.

One of the best things I did for my sons when they were in elementary school was to enforce a nightly reading routine. Just like they had to take a bath and brush their teeth each night, they also HAD to read. The rule was they had to go to bed 30 minutes early each night during the school year and read. So, if their bedtime was 8:00, they knew they had to get in bed at 7:30 and read. Always. Every night.

I would leave their door open to make sure they were actually reading too. It wasn't 30 minutes to continue playing. They were supposed to be in bed reading during that time, and I frequently checked on them. It's not that I didn't trust them, but—well, okay I didn't trust them.

While that worked during the school year, it didn't work in the summer when they stayed up later. So in the summer, I would make them lie or sit in the living room in the middle of the day and read for 30 minutes. I would set the timer, and they were not allowed to get up until the timer went off. Sometimes I would read with them, or sometimes I would be cooking dinner. However, I kept them close so I could make sure they were indeed reading.

To be honest, my boys didn't like it in the beginning. They complained a lot, but I continued to make them read every day anyway. Eventually, their complaints stopped because they knew I was dead set on having them read daily. By third grade, however, they really started to enjoy reading and I no longer had to force them. By sixth grade, they were both reading on a post-high school level. They both did very well in school and on their ACT scores, and I attribute most of it to them being excellent readers.

I want to add that even though I made them practice reading on their own, I also continued to read aloud to them. I tried to choose great chapter books that were highly recommended. I remember being totally exhausted at the end of the day as they begged me to read just one more chapter of an exciting book.

Here's one final bonus to having your children read daily. Did you know if your children make a certain score on their college entrance exams (ACT or SAT), they will automatically get scholarship money? Two universities in my state award $10,000 or more to students scoring high on their ACT exams. Do you know one of the best ways to score high on those exams? READ! Students who are well-read, score much higher than those who aren't. So if you're lacking motivation to get your children to read daily, think $10,000! That should be great motivation!

Independent Play

As discussed in Chapter 11, children need lots of unstructured, independent play. Play is one of the basic ways children develop and strengthen their mental and physical ability.

So make sure your children have *at least* an hour or two a day of independent play. Independent play does not include watching TV, playing video games, or using any type of technology. This is time where children learn to play and entertain themselves.

For children who have never learned to play and entertain

themselves, start slowly. Initially, you may only want to have independent playtime for about 15 minutes. Gradually build up the time they spend playing to an hour or two a day. Use the timer and tell them they have to play independently until the timer goes off.

Scheduling independent playtime into your children's routine doesn't mean you never play with your children. I played with my kids most every day. However, I played in moderation, and the rest of the time I expected my children to entertain themselves.

Outside Play

When I was growing up, mothers would send their children out to play with strict instructions not to come home until dinner. We rode our bikes. We played in the creek. We walked to the park. In fact, we played outside most of the day.

I am sadly aware that times are different. In many areas, it's not even safe to let your kids be alone outside. However, if you live in an area that is safe, add outside playtime to your routine. Playing outside is good for children!

I was blessed to live in a safe neighborhood when my boys were growing up. I also had a fenced-in backyard for my boys to play in when they were toddlers. Every day, I made my boys play outside. When it was cold, I bundled them up. It wasn't long before I saw them throw off their coats because they got hot from running. In the summer, I sent them out to play in the sprinklers. I sent them out in the rain in raincoats, galoshes, and umbrellas. I sent them out in the snow in snowsuits. They loved outside time! To this day, my grown sons love to be outside. They love to golf, jog, hike, fish, play sports, etc. In fact, they hate to be cooped up inside all day.

Homework Routine

Since every child is different, let your children set their own schedule for doing homework. Some like to relax after school and not do homework until much later. Others like to get it over. It really doesn't matter. However, if they procrastinate and don't do it, then you get to set the schedule. Your schedule might just comprise of no playing or television until the homework is finished.

Clean-Up Routine

Make clean-up time part of your daily routine. I'm not talking about deep cleaning your house on a weeknight. I'm talking about getting your children into a habit of picking up their toys and things before they get ready for bed. This will train your kids to pick up after themselves and help develop a sense of orderliness. If they're old enough, I encourage you to have the whole family help clean the kitchen after dinner as well.

Adding clean-up time to your daily routine will help instill the unselfish lesson that everyone has to do their part. This isn't about having a clean house. (Although that's a happy by-product.) Implementing a clean-up time is about training your children to be helpful and kind to others. (It's not kind to make someone else do all the work!)

Be ultra-organized. Have a place for everything. Get some sort of container or two to put their toys each night.

If you think having your children clean up each night would take more like two hours instead of five minutes, let me make a suggestion: Don't have so many toys out at once. Instead, put only a few toys out at a time and then rotate them weekly or monthly.

I used to believe if I had lots of toys for my boys, they would spend hours playing with them. Instead, they would just scatter their toys all over the floor. Then they would wander off looking for something to do. The room was so cluttered with toys, there was no room to play. And instead of finding a toy and figuring out how it worked, they would pick it up for about a second and move on. The clutter was overwhelming! They couldn't concentrate on any one thing. Clean-up seemed impossible.

Then I read about rotating the toys. I put all my toys in clear lawn bags, numbered them, and put them in the attic. I had twelve bags of toys! Then I would take only one sack of toys out at a time. All the toys could fit in one toy basket, making clean-up a breeze. I noticed instead of moving from one toy to the next, the boys actually started concentrating on one specific toy. Without the clutter, there was lots of room to play, run around, push the corn popper, and build with blocks. Before I got out a new bag of toys, I put all the old toys back in a lawn sack, numbered it, and put it back in the attic. Because the boys only saw the toys once every three months, it was like getting a new sack of toys each week. I used to get a new sack of toys out on a day when I was really busy. They would get so excited about their "new" toys, they would play for hours.

Bedtime Routine

The first rule of a bedtime routine is to go to bed at approximately the same time each night. That way if your children argue or want to stay up later, you just say, "No. Bedtime is at 8:00. That's the rule." Make it a fact of life and there will be little room for argument. Of course, there will be occasional exceptions but try to make those exceptions rare.

What time to put your children to bed is up to you. Many working parents like to keep their kids up later so they can spend more time with them. If a later bedtime works for the family, that's fine. But don't feel guilty if you want to put the kids to bed early. Babies, children, and teens need significantly more sleep than adults. Their brains and bodies are developing rapidly. Plus, without adequate sleep, children will be more prone to crankiness and irritability during the day. Here's a general guideline to how many hours of sleep children require.

Age	Recommended
0-3 months	14-17 hours
4-11 months	12-15 hours
1-2 years	11-14 hours
3-5 years	10-13 hours
6-13 years	9-11 hours
14-17 years	8-10 hours

Not only are children less cranky and irritable with an early bedtime, but there's an added bonus: Parents get some quiet time with their spouse and time to unwind from working all day. While many parents feel they need to spend more time with their children, they also need to make sure to spend time alone with their spouse. One of the most important things you can do for your children is to give them a secure family life where they know Mom loves Dad, and Dad loves Mom.

Once you've established the bedtime, figure out how long it will take your children to get ready for bed and start getting ready accordingly. For instance, if bedtime is at 8:00 and it takes 10 minutes to clean-up, and 30 minutes to bathe, brush teeth, and put on pajamas, then start getting ready at 7:20.

Getting into a bedtime ritual helps children prepare for bedtime. By doing the same thing each night, they know bedtime is coming. Whether you want to get in the habit of reading each night or praying, get into a routine and try to stick to it. As a word of caution, you might not want to get into a complicated routine whereby you won't have time to do it every night. Keep it simple so if you do have to be out late, you can quickly put them to bed without a long, drawn-out ritual. Our bedtime routine simply consisted of clean-up time, taking a bath, brushing teeth, putting on pajamas, saying a prayer, and kissing goodnight. (I had read to them earlier in the day.)

If your children have trouble going to sleep quickly, consider allowing them to leave their light on for 30 minutes or more so they can look at a book. (Not a glowing screen!) But they need to stay in their beds to unwind. Having them stay in their bed even when they want to get up, will help develop their self-control.

14
BABY AND TODDLER DISCIPLINE

For most parents, having children is one of life's greatest joys. But it can also be one of life's biggest challenges. You can save yourself a lot of headaches if you train your children to obey before the age of two. If you can master that, the rest of childhood will be a whole lot easier.

Unfortunately, many parents think obedience in the first two years is unrealistic. The common strategy today is to redirect toddlers' attention when they misbehave. In other words, distract them from their bad behavior by offering something else interesting to do. For instance, if your toddler picks up your cell phone, you give her a toy and say, "Here, let's play with this toy instead of the phone." While redirection is a good technique for some circumstances, it shouldn't be your only method. How in the world are your children going to learn to obey if you constantly ignore their poor behavior and distract them instead? If you simply redirect and distract every time your children do a no-no, your children will never learn to obey.

Along this same line of thinking, another approach is just to tolerate the toddler years. The reasoning goes that children will eventually outgrow their poor behavior. But if you think this "difficult phase" will just pass, think again. While children might outgrow some of their impulsive and childish behavior, they probably will not outgrow an attitude of disobedience.

I have repeatedly asked parents who have wonderfully behaved children their secret. The answer was almost invariably the same: Teach your children to obey before they are two. You must lay a strong foundation of obedience in the pre-toddler years. It's not easy, and it takes diligence. But if you work hard the first two years, it will save you lots of stress and headaches in later years.

Does this mean your children will obey you each and every time you speak by age two? Unfortunately, no. But by having age two as a goal, you're laying the groundwork for obedience. It may take the entire second year to get your children to consistently obey, but by age three, you should start to see consistent obedience.

Start Early – Around Seven Months of Age

The secret, however, is not to wait until your child is two. Discipline must start much earlier—around seven months of age. This is the time to start teaching your baby the basic commands of obedience.

Remember, the root word of discipline is disciple, which means "to train." If you want well-behaved children, your focus should be on training correct behavior. Your babies have absolutely no idea what they should and should not do. It's your job to teach them.

Author Burton L. White, in his book *Raising a Happy, Unspoiled Child*, contends that if you don't have your babies under control by the time they are 14 months old, you're headed for those terrible twos. Under control means: Do they lie still for you while being diapered? Do they hit and kick? Do they take no for an answer? Basic obedience should be established by even this young age.

One of the biggest problems parents have with disciplining their pre-toddlers is they are unclear on exactly what their babies can and cannot understand. After all, if they can't understand, it's not fair to reprimand them. But most babies can understand long before they can speak. And even before babies can understand your words, they understand the tone of your voice. Somewhere between six and nine months, most babies will understand the word no, with seven-and-a-half months being about the average age. If your babies continue to act like they don't understand you by age one, consider getting their hearing checked, or consult a pediatrician.

The preschool years are the time to lay the foundation of effective discipline—love. Babies and toddlers need lots and lots of love! They need to be held, kissed, cuddled and talked to a lot. They need a childproof area where they can play and explore. But this is also the time to lay the basic foundation of obedience. If you don't have a strong foundation in the toddler years, future discipline will be an uphill struggle.

Basic Commands of Obedience

There are seven fundamental commands that you need to train your children to obey by the time they are 18 months of age. Being able to obey these basic commands is the foundation of obedience. However, obedience will not be learned overnight, so start early. The basic commands are:

1. No. Do not touch.
2. Come here.
3. Sit down. (Such as in the grocery cart or highchair.)
4. Go. (Such as go to your room, get in your highchair.)
5. Stay. (Such as right beside you in a store.)
6. Stop.
7. Lie still. (Such as when you change a diaper.)

Somewhere between five to seven months, work on teaching your children the first command, "No. Do not touch." After that, begin teaching the other commands as they occur.

So how do you teach these basic commands? With Mini-Training Sessions of course! For example, if you want to teach your children the first command, "No. Do not touch," here's what you might do:

Train your children that when you say, "No. Do not touch," they need to:

1. Look at you.
2. Clasp both their hands together.

This will take their attention off the forbidden object and give them something specific to do—clasp their hands together. Every time they do it correctly, be sure to get excited and reward them with hugs and kisses.

So let's say your baby is about to touch your cell phone and you say, "No. Do not touch." Next ask, "What are you supposed to do?" You might walk over to them and physically move their face to look at you, and then clasp their little hands together. Remember to praise them when they do the right thing.

For the command "Come here," have them practice coming to you when you call. Make a game of it. When they come, hug, kiss, and tell them how proud you are that they obeyed.

Mini-Training Sessions shouldn't be long—probably less than a minute. However, do practice these basic commands of obedience often throughout the day.

Consequences for Pre-toddlers

While the consequences for babies and toddlers may differ slightly, the basic philosophy of discipline applies. First, make sure your children know the rule, such as "Do not touch the trashcan." Then, if they disobey, they need to have an immediate consequence. For babies and toddlers, the consequence needs to be immediate or not at all. So as soon as it's clear they understand the basic command, each time they disobey they need to have a consequence.

Remember though, consequences are not appropriate for accidents, mistakes, or exploring new things.

There are essentially four consequences you can use on pre-toddlers:

- Verbal Correction
- Take Away Object of Misbehavior
- Time-out
- Slight Swat on Hand

Verbal Correction

The first consequence is a verbal correction. This simply means to scold, such as "No. Do not touch the TV." In the beginning, when you are first training your babies to obey a basic command, begin by giving the instruction. If they don't obey, give them a verbal correction and physically move them to make them obey. For instance, let's say you told your baby not to touch the TV, yet he touches it. Say, "No. Do not touch the TV." Then pick him up and remove him from the forbidden object. Or let's say the instruction was to "Come here." If he doesn't respond, give a verbal correction and physically go and get him.

However, after teaching your children a basic command and they disobey, they need to have an additional consequence.

Take Away the Object of Misbehavior

The second consequence is to take away whatever object they are using to misbehave. For instance, if they are banging their spoon on their highchair, after one warning, take it away. (Don't forget to use if-then statements. *If* you bang your spoon again, *then* I'm going to take it away.) If they're knocking their car against the wall, give them one warning and then take it away. Taking away their precious possession would be their consequence for disobedience.

Time-out

Time-out is the third consequence. For this consequence, babies are removed from the no-no and put into time-out for approximately 1 to 4 minutes. A playpen placed in another room, or the child's crib is an ideal place for time-out for the pre-toddler. During time-out, toys and blankies should be off limits. For children under 15 months, it is recommended that children be put in time-out for no more than 5 minutes. Generally, 2 to 3 minutes is enough. Be sure to set the timer as soon as you put them in time-out so you don't forget!

For example, if your child is not supposed to touch the blinds and he does, first verbally correct him. Say, "No. Do not touch the blinds." If he does it again, say no again and physically put him in his playpen or crib with no toys or blankets. Then get out of his sight. In 2 to 4 minutes, let him out to play. If he touches the blinds again, repeat the verbal correction and the time-out. Repeat as often as necessary.

Some might disagree that blankies should be off limits during time-out. However, for toddlers, time-out is never more than 5 minutes. Therefore, I think it's acceptable to take away their blankie for that short time period. Time-out should not be a pleasant experience.

If you're concerned that your children might associate their crib with a place of punishment, don't be. Your approach to how you place your babies there will be totally different and they'll understand. When you place them in the crib to sleep, you use a loving, sweet voice and hug, kiss, and cover them up with their blanket before leaving. When you put them in the crib for time-out, you're giving them a verbal correction and taking away their blanket. The difference will be obvious.

For older toddlers who can crawl out of a playpen or crib, consider putting a childproof doorknob guard on the inside of their bedroom door. Or you could cut their bedroom door in half to create a "Dutch" door like they have at nurseries. Hang both halves up, and put the doorknob on the outside of the bottom door. This way your children can't get out, yet you can easily check on them. I always wanted to do this to my sons' bedroom door but never did because I didn't want to mess up the door. However, by the time my twins were school-age, their door was so dinged up they needed a new door anyway!

Time-out or isolation is also good when toddlers are whiny or won't take no for an answer. For instance, suppose your child wants you to play with her while you're fixing dinner. You say no, but she keeps asking over and over. Say, "I said no. Don't ask me again. If you ask me again, I'm going to put you in your room for time-out." Then, if she asks you again, immediately put her in her room. It may take a couple of scenarios like that, but she'll eventually figure out you're not kidding.

Slight Swat on Hand

The last option is a swat on the hand. The swat should involve a slight sting but obviously shouldn't hurt your children. A swat on the hand should always be accompanied with a verbal correction. So if your baby touches the lamp after you've taught him not to, say, "No. Do not touch." Then swat his little hand.

I can already hear the gasps of horror at the thought of swatting a pre-toddler's hand. I am not talking about beating children! I'm suggesting that when your pre-toddlers *intentionally* disobey, you swat their little hand—just enough to give a slight sting.

Many would argue that physical punishment should never be used. Instead, give explanations. But reasoning and explanations are not for toddlers. They don't have the mental capabilities to understand parental reason and logic.

Children of this age are motivated through concrete consequences. They behave the way they do on the basis of rewards and punishments and not with moral reasoning or logic. Can you imagine a toddler

134

saying, "You mean the reason I can't touch the DVR is because I might break it? Oh, that makes sense. I won't touch it again." They don't care if they break it! They do care, however, if they have an unpleasant consequence that directly affects them.

If you're concerned that a swat on the hand will teach your children to hit, don't worry. A swat on the hand does not promote violence. It promotes self-control. And for those who would suggest that a slight swat on the hand is equivalent to child abuse, that is irresponsible and untruthful. A swat on the hand done by loving parents who are using it to stop their child from wrong behavior is not child abuse. It's not even close. Child abuse is venting hostility and frustration toward a child. The other is for love of the child. Abuse is a horrible thing—but so is not disciplining your children.

Allow me to share a true, anecdotal story. I once taught with a woman who was so sweet. The students and staff loved her. When her daughter was two, her husband's mother remarried a child psychologist who counseled parents how to raise their children. On one visit to her new in-law's home, her daughter disobeyed. My friend swatted her daughter's little hand. Her new in-law went ballistic! He went off on how you should never hit a child and that she was going to damage her child psychologically, etc. My friend was devastated that a parenting "expert" had told her she was teaching her daughter to hit and be violent. That night, with tears in her eyes, she asked her husband, "Do you really think that I've damaged our child because I swatted her hand?" Her husband replied, "Let's examine the results of his parenting advice. He has two grown sons in their late twenties. Both sons are unemployed, alcoholics, and on drugs. Hmmm. Do you really want to take advice from that parenting "expert?"

First-Time Obedience

As mentioned in Chapter 5, train your children to have first-time obedience. It's just as easy to teach them to obey the first time as it is to obey the fourth time. When you give an instruction, expect them to obey immediately. If they don't, they should get an immediate consequence. If you train your children from the beginning to obey at once, they will. By teaching them to obey immediately, you're also developing their self-control—the same self-control needed for other virtues of integrity

It's very important in these early years to let your children know that you are in charge, not them. While they can certainly make little decisions, they need to learn early that you make the final decisions. If you don't establish early who the boss is, they will constantly test you and struggle for power.

TV, Technology, and Your Preschooler

As discussed in Chapter 10, the American Academy of Pediatrics recommends absolutely no screen time for babies under 18 months old. For toddlers 18 to 24 months old, the AAP recommends no screen time unless watched with an adult who explains what the child is seeing. In other words, don't allow a toddler to watch media alone. (Many pediatricians and researchers recommend no screen time for children under the age of three.) For children age two to five, the AAP recommends no more than one hour of media per day.

Remember, the absolute best thing for babies' mental and physical development is to talk to them frequently and let them play. No educational technology can compete with that.

But how are you supposed to get anything done without the TV to babysit? Well, you could do it the old-fashioned way. If you need to make dinner, have your preschoolers come in the kitchen with you. Let them play with your pots and pans or plastic storage containers. Or have them bring their toys into the kitchen and play while you make dinner. That way, you can talk to them while they play. (A double learning experience!) Tell them everything you're doing as you make dinner. If they're old enough, have them "help" you make dinner. Having your children in the kitchen while you cook is a great opportunity for conversation.

If you need to take a shower, put your baby in a playpen or in their room for independent play. Teach your children to entertain themselves. If you can accomplish that, you won't need to turn on the TV for entertainment.

15
THE OUT-OF-CONTROL CHILD

What if your children are older and you didn't know to do any of this? Don't worry. There's more than one way to do everything. Just because you didn't do it my way, doesn't mean your way wasn't great too. Some new parents put their newborns on a rigid feeding schedule. Some feed on-demand. Generally, both sets swear by their method. If your method of discipline is working, that's great. Stick with it.

But what if your children are older and your methods haven't been working? First, don't beat yourself up, and don't feel guilty. No one is a perfect parent. We've all made mistakes—and lots of them! And even if you were a great parent, sometimes kids just don't turn out as we hoped.

Don't dwell on your mistakes or the past. Instead, resolve to do your best today. Kids can change! Once they figure out that they can't get away with their bad behavior, they'll stop.

Think about all the out-of-control boys who are sent to marine boot camps at age 18. After 12 weeks, most are completely changed. They couldn't get away with their nonsense at boot camp. (I suspect their drill sergeant didn't have the tender heart of a mother.)

I once had a student named Adam. He had a reputation for throwing himself down and having full-fledged tantrums. His mother told me about it the first day of school. She said there was nothing she could do about it. I made it perfectly clear in the beginning that I would not allow it. Adam tried it on me a few times, but it got him nowhere. I expected good behavior, and I absolutely would not put up with

137

tantrums. The result was that after a month, he never threw a tantrum with me again. However, he continued throwing tantrums at home. His mother just didn't have the fortitude to stop it.

What's my point? Your children can change when they finally realize that you absolutely, positively won't put up with their misbehavior anymore.

So how exactly do you go about implementing a new discipline policy with an older child? First, remember a loving relationship with your children is essential. Your children will not yield to your newfound authority unless they know you're doing this out of love. Tell them you love them every day! Be affectionate if they'll allow it. Write them love notes. Be the adult, and even if they get rude and hostile, calmly express your unconditional love.

Second, develop a game plan. Plan exactly what the new rules are and what the consequences will be for breaking those rules. Write your new discipline policy in a Behavior Contract so your kids will know the exact rules and the exact consequences. (See chapter 9.) Then, plan for every contingency. For instance, what if you lay down the law and they don't pay attention to you? What are you going to do? Have it all planned out so you'll be prepared and won't react emotionally.

If you've got a spouse, be sure to be in this together. Present a united front. If you're a single parent, get help. Changing an out-of-control child is emotionally draining. You need support. If you have a father, brother, relative, or neighbor who could help, take it. Let me caution, however, to find someone whose children turned out well. If their kids didn't turn out successfully, why would you seek their counsel?

Single moms especially need the help of a good male role model if they have a son. Boys need a strong male figure in their lives during their teenage years. I was fine when my boys were young. But when they turned into teenagers, I needed my husband! My heart was way too tender to give the firmness needed in the teen years. My husband, on the other hand, didn't care if he made our sons mad. If they broke the rules, they got in trouble. He gave them boundaries that were consistently enforced, and that was exactly what they needed.

When my boys were in high school, we had a neighbor who was a single mom. Her teenage son was being rude and disrespectful to her. Her discipline techniques no longer seemed to work. So she asked for help from my husband. My husband had a long talk with her son. He basically said: "If I ever hear that you're disrespectful to your mom, you're going to have to deal with me. Your mom has given me full permission to do whatever I need to do to get you to be respectful. I will not allow you to treat your mother like that." He then went on to tell the boy exactly what he was going to do. (Sorry, but the details of this are fairly politically incorrect.) The mom reported that her son completely turned around. She said she only had to mention my husband's name before he straightened out. My husband never had to make good on his threat. The boy knew from my sons that my husband meant what he said and would definitely enforce the consequences. (By the way, that boy is now in medical school!)

Once you've got a plan and a support team, sit down with your children and have a heart-to-heart talk. Let them know that in the past, you have made some mistakes as a parent, but starting right now, you want to be a good, responsible parent. And that means setting limits and consistently enforcing them. Then proceed to tell them the exact rules and the exact consequences.

Be aware that they will test you. They have gotten away with misbehavior in the past, and they probably think they can continue to do so. So be prepared. Know exactly what you're going to do if they break a rule, and then do it! There's no need to yell or scream. Just do exactly what you said you would do. If you let them slide even a little bit, and don't back up what you said you would do, it just tells them that you really didn't mean what you said. They'll know in their heart that if they just keep pushing you, they can eventually wear you down.

Bear in mind, it will get much worse before it gets better. Your children are used to getting their way and doing what they want. They're not used to losing, and they won't take it lying down. They will probably fight you every step of the way. But you must wear them down before they wear you down. Also, don't put it past them to manipulate you by using guilt or sympathy. They'll try anything to regain the control they had over you.

To gain control over your out-of-control children, you're going to have to do something that you won't want to do—make them terribly unhappy. Yes, they are absolutely going to hate your new discipline policy. So be prepared for complaining. But remember, being good parents doesn't mean making your children continually happy. In fact, good parents will probably make their children unhappy some of the time. It's unpleasant not getting your way and having to do things that you don't want to do. Things that are good for you often do not make you too happy. So don't be distressed to see your children upset over this situation. It just has to be done.

This is why you need a good support team. You need friends and family who will encourage you that you're doing the right thing. It's also helpful for your support team to back you up in front of your children. Let your kids see that their dealing with a team of adults who are united.

Again, let me caution you in the selection of your support team. If you have friends or relatives who are too permissive or can't bear to see a child upset, they shouldn't be on your support team. I know I couldn't even talk to certain relatives about some of the consequences we gave my son Hunter during his teen years. They thought we were being way too hard on him. Thank goodness I didn't listen to them!

Be realistic though. There is no quick fix for children who have had a lifetime of being out of control. You can't just try this advice for a few days, and then conclude it doesn't work. It won't happen overnight. In fact, the longer the bad habits have prevailed, the longer it's going to take to correct. It's like losing weight. It didn't take a week to put on those extra pounds, and it's not going to take a week to get them off.

Don't get discouraged if you digress. Just like going off a diet, if you blow it one day, don't give up altogether. Just start fresh and new the next day.

If all of this sounds discouraging, let me end with a wonderful success story. I know this story well, because it's about my son Hunter.

Hunter fit every definition of a strong-willed child. He was born mad and just had a difficult personality. I remember calling my husband at work one day when Hunter was three months old. I said in tears, "I don't think Hunter likes me." My husband tried to cheer me up by saying, "Don't worry, Honey. Hunter doesn't like anyone." (His twin brother Skyler, on the other hand, was so sweet!) While Hunter was well behaved in the early years, it certainly wasn't easy. It didn't help matters that I got a divorce from their father when they were 10, and remarried and moved to a different city when they were 12. So when Hunter turned 13, he turned awful. Hunter was disrespectful, disobedient, and downright hard to live with. I was frequently reminded of the Mark Twain quote: "When a boy turns 13, put him in a barrel and feed him through a knot hole. When he turns 16, plug up the hole."

I cried so many tears during that time. It seemed like the nicer I was to him, the meaner he was to me. Now he wasn't disrespectful to my new husband, Roger. Roger wouldn't have put up with it! We finally had to get really tough on Hunter. Here are just a few of the things we did to him:

- He only had a $30 basic cell phone. It had no data plan and it did not text. (His twin brother had a really nice phone.)
- One day while Hunter was at school, my husband and I packed up everything of Hunter's except his bed and clothes. We rented a storage unit for 6 months and put all of his stuff in there—although he didn't know what happened to his stuff. We took his bike, skateboard, Game Boy, iPod, literally everything.
- If he became disrespectful or broke rules, he was sent to his room. (There was nothing in it!)
- After lying to us, Hunter was grounded in his empty room until he memorized 26 scriptures about lying.
- My husband left out brochures of military schools around the house for Hunter to see.
- My husband used to tell Hunter that the only thing we had to provide was food, clothes, and shelter. Hunter thought that meant we had to provide mall clothes from Abercrombie. My husband said, "No, You're getting your clothes at Wal Mart."

Inflicting those consequences on Hunter was pure agony for me. I hated upsetting my child. But my husband was strong, and he enforced our rules. (Note: Even though we enforced the deserved consequences, we always conveyed our love for him.)

When Hunter was almost 16, he broke nearly every one of our rules—all in one night! His consequence was he got no driver's license and no car until he turned 17—which was a year away. That was hard, particularly since his twin brother got both his license and a car. Skyler drove to high school each morning. Hunter had to ride the bus with the middle schoolers. They made fun of his basic phone.

With that last consequence, my husband had finally convinced Hunter that his rebellion just wasn't worth the horrible consequence that he most certainly would incur. Starting at age 16, Hunter became wonderful. He was respectful, hardworking, and responsible. We started calling him our "Golden Boy." Today, Hunter is one of the nicest young men you'll ever meet. He is so kind, honest, and respectful. We have a great relationship. I'm so glad that we showed him some tough love during his teen years.

So don't get discouraged, and don't give up. My son Hunter is living proof that even a snarky, strong-willed teenager can be changed into a loving, well-mannered young adult

NOTES

Page   Chapter 10: The Effect of TV and Technology on a Growing Child's Brain

87   *The evidence of negative effects:* Radesky, J., & Christakis, D. (2016). Media and Young Minds. *Pediatrics, 138*(5). Retrieved from http://pediatrics.aappublications.org/content/138/5/e20162591

87   *no screen time for children under age 3:* Boseley, S. (2012, October 08). Ban Under-Threes from Watching Television, Says Study. *The Guardian.* Retrieved from https://www.theguardian.com/society/2012/oct/09/ban-under-threes-watching-television

87   *no interactive screen time before the age of 10:* Kardaras, N. (2016, December 17). Kids Turn Violent as Parents Battle 'Digital Heroin' Addiction. *New York Post.* Retrieved from http://nypost.com/2016/12/17/kids-turn-violent-as-parents-battle-digital-heroin-addiction/

87   *In 2008, France actually banned:* Alleyne, R. (2008, August 21). France Bans Marketing Television Programmes Targeted at Under Threes. *The Telegraph.* Retrieved from http://www.telegraph.co.uk/news/worldnews/europe/france/2595495/France-bans-marketing-television-programmes-targeted-at-under-threes.html

87   *For children age 2 to 5:* Radesky, J., & Christakis, D. (2016). Media and Young Minds. *Pediatrics, 138*(5). Retrieved from http://pediatrics.aappublications.org/content/138/5/e20162591

88   *In her book, Endangered Minds:* Healy, J. M. (1990). *Endangered Minds: Why Our Children Don't Think.* New York: Simon and Schuster.

88   *Students from elementary schools to universities:* DeSilver, D. (2015, February 02). U.S. Students Improving - Slowly - in Math and Science, but Still Lagging Internationally. Retrieved from http://www.pewresearch.org/fact-tank/2015/02/02/u-s-students-improving-slowly-in-math-and-science-but-still-lagging-internationally

88   *According to a 2013 U.S. Department of Education study:* Crum, M. (2014, December 12). The U.S. Illiteracy Rate Hasn't Changed In 10 Years. *The Huffington Post.* Retrieved from http://www.huffingtonpost.com/2013/09/06/illiteracy-rate_n_3880355.html

88   *The National Institute for Literacy reports:* National Institute for Literacy, National Center for Adult Literacy, & U.S. Census Bureau. (n.d.). Staggering Illiteracy Statistics. Retrieved from http://literacyprojectfoundation.org/community/statistics/

88   *the scores of the Scholastic Aptitude Test:* Winn, M. (1977). *The Plug-in Drug* (p. 82). New York: Viking Press.

88   *their brains are not developing properly:* Yapp, R. (2014, January 10). Children Who Watch Too Much TV May Have 'Damaged Brain Structures'. *Daily Mail.* Retrieved from http://www.dailymail.co.uk/health/article-2537240/Children-watch-TV-damaged-brain-structures.html

88   *their brains are not developing properly:* Fields, D. (2015, May 4). Watching TV Alters Children's Brain Structure and Lowers IQ. Retrieved from http://blog.brainfacts.org/2015/05/watching-tv-alters-childrens-brain-structure-and-lowers-iq/#.WIgVb1x2F2g

88   *their brains are not developing properly:* Fields, R. D. (2015, December 14). Does TV Rot Your Brain? Retrieved from https://www.scientificamerican.com/article/does-tv-rot-your-brain/

88   *The first 3 years of a child's life:* The Urban Child institute. (2016, April 4). Infants, Toddlers and Television. Retrieved from http://www.urbanchildinstitute.org/articles/policy-briefs/infants-toddlers-and-television

88   *The power of a neuron:* Kolari, J. (2012, April 04). How Parenting Affects Your Child's Brain [Video file]. Retrieved from https://www.youtube.com/watch?v=uFckNenV-QE

88   *In order to have a "good" brain:* Healy, J. M. (1990). *Endangered Minds: Why Our Children Don't Think* (pp. 208-209). New York: Simon and Schuster.

88   *However, a baby is born with:* Walsh, D. A. (2012). *Smart Parenting, Smarter Kids: The One Brain Book You Need to Help Your Child Grow Brighter, Healthier, and Happier* (p. 88). New York: Free Press.

88   *But it's the connections that form in early childhood:* Graham, J., & Forstadt, L. (n.d.). Children and Brain Development: What We Know About How Children Learn. Retrieved from https://extension.umaine.edu/publications/4356e

89   *These neural connections are made in two ways:* Walsh, D. (2008, May 08). *Brain Power* [Video file]. Retrieved from https://www.youtube.com/watch?v=6f8NdC9Amhg

89   *It is the activities children experience:* Walsh, D. (2008, May 08). *Brain Power* [Video file]. Retrieved from https://www.youtube.com/watch?v=6f8NdC9Amhg

89   *It is the activities children experience:* Graham, J., & Forstadt, L. (n.d.). Children and Brain Development: What We Know About How Children Learn. Retrieved from https://extension.umaine.edu/publications/4356e

89   *It is the activities children experience:* Christakis, D. *How TV Affects the Brains of Young Children* [Video file]. Retrieved February 05, 2012, from https://www.youtube.com/watch?v=v2SdEpHjrjw

89   *Research has shown that the most important factor:* Healy, J. M. (1990). *Endangered Minds: Why Our Children Don't Think* (p. 91). New York: Simon and Schuster.

89   *Neuropsychologist Alexander Luria:* Luria, A. R. (1981). *Language and Cognition*. Washington, D.C.: V.H. Winston.

89   *Watching too much TV can actually delay a child's language:* Zimmerman, F. J., Christakis, D. A., & Meltzoff, A. N. (2007). Associations between Media Viewing and Language Development in Children Under Age 2 Years. *The Journal of Pediatrics, 151*(4), 364-368. doi:10.1016/j.jpeds.2007.04.071

89   *Watching too much TV can actually delay a child's language:* Hill, D. (2016, October 21). Why to Avoid TV for Infants & Toddlers. Retrieved from https://www.healthychildren.org/English/family-life/Media/Pages/Why-to-Avoid-TV-Before-Age-2.aspx

89   *Watching too much TV can actually delay a child's language:* Fields, D. (2015, May 4). Watching TV Alters Children's Brain Structure and Lowers IQ. Retrieved from http://blog.brainfacts.org/2015/05/watching-tv-alters-childrens-brain-structure-and-lowers-iq/#.WIgVb1x2F2g

89   *most children's programs are mainly visual:* Calvert, S. L., Huston, A. C., Watkins, B. A., & Wright, J. C. (1982). The Relation between Selective Attention to Television Forms and Children's Comprehension of Content. *Child Development, 53*(3), 601. doi:10.2307/1129371

89   *Plus, the language centers:* Walsh, D. A. (2012). *Smart Parenting, Smarter Kids: The One Brain Book You Need to Help Your Child Grow Brighter, Healthier, and Happier*. New York: Free Press.

89   *It is conversation, not listening to media:* Dewar, G. (2015, March). The Effects of Television on Language Skills. Retrieved from http://www.parentingscience.com/effects-of-television-on-children-learning-speech.html

90   *This practice talking helps to:* Healy, J. M. (1990). *Endangered Minds: Why Our Children Don't Think*. New York: Simon and Schuster.

90   *This practice talking will eventually:* Healy, J. M. (1990). *Endangered Minds: Why Our Children Don't Think* (p. 249). New York: Simon and Schuster

90   *This practice talking will eventually:* Tullett, A. M., & Inzlicht, M. (2010). The Voice of Self-control: Blocking the Inner Voice Increases Impulsive Responding. *Acta Psychologica, 135*(2), 252-256. doi:10.1016/j.actpsy.2010.07.008

90   *The second way to develop:* Walsh, D. A. (2012). *Smart Parenting, Smarter Kids: The One Brain Book You Need to Help Your Child Grow Brighter, Healthier, and Happier*. New York: Free Press.

90   *Play develops:* Bay Area Early Childhood Funders. (2007). Play in the Early Years: Key to

School Success, A Policy Brief. Retrieved from
http://earlychildhoodfunders.org/pdf/play07.pdf

91 *Researchers have found that brain connections in animals:* Eisenberg, A., Murkoff, H. E., &
Hathaway, S. E. (1994). *What to Expect the Toddler Years* (p. 55). New York: Workman Pub.

91 *Play also develops good verbal:* 15. Bay Area Early Childhood Funders. (2007). Play in the Early
Years: Key to School Success, A Policy Brief. Retrieved from
http://earlychildhoodfunders.org/pdf/play07.pdf

91 *Instead, it establishes strong, overbuilt connections:* Healy, J. M. (1990). *Endangered Minds: Why Our
Children Don't Think* (p. 216). New York: Simon and Schuster

91 *Instead, it establishes strong, overbuilt connections:* Emery, M., & Emery, F. (1980). The Vacuous
Vision: The TV Medium. *Journal of the University Film Association, 32*(1/2), 27-31. Retrieved
from Stable URL: http://www.jstor.org/stable/20687503

91 *And, if neural pathways are not developed:* Graham, J., & Forstadt, L. (n.d.). Children and Brain
Development: What We Know About How Children Learn. Retrieved from
https://extension.umaine.edu/publications/4356e

92 *Since mental effort develops the prefrontal:* Healy, J. M. (1990). *Endangered Minds: Why Our Children
Don't Think* (p. 216). New York: Simon and Schuster

92 *But without full development of the prefrontal functions:* Healy, J. M. (1990). *Endangered Minds: Why
Our Children Don't Think.* New York: Simon and Schuster.

92 *Not only does watching TV hinder their mental:* Bergland, C. (2013, November 23). One More
Reason to Unplug Your Television. *Psychology Today.* Retrieved from
https://www.psychologytoday.com/blog/the-athletes-way/201311/one-more-reason-
unplug-your-television

92 *Not only does watching TV hinder their mental:* Canadian Paediatric Society. (2003). Impact of
Media Use on Children and Youth. Retrieved from
https://www.ncbi.nlm.nih.gov/pmc/articles/PMC2792691/

92 *A good brain for learning:* Healy, J. M. (1990). *Endangered Minds: Why Our Children Don't Think*
(p. 216). New York: Simon and Schuster

92 *causes both hemispheres to shrink:* Bergland, C. (2013, November 23). One More Reason to
Unplug Your Television. *Psychology Today.* Retrieved from
https://www.psychologytoday.com/blog/the-athletes-way/201311/one-more-reason-
unplug-your-television

92 *The left hemisphere manages:* Melina, R. (2011, January 12). What's the Difference Between the
Right Brain and Left Brain? Retrieved from http://www.livescience.com/32935-whats-the-
difference-between-the-right-brain-and-left-brain.html

93 *The left hemisphere is processed through hearing:* Healy, J. M. (1990). *Endangered Minds: Why Our
Children Don't Think* (pp.125, 210). New York: Simon and Schuster

93 *Television for young children is mainly visual:* Winn, M. (1977). *The Plug-in Drug* (pp. 42, 47). New
York: Viking Press.

93 *right brain activity increases:* Moore, W. (2001). Television: Opiate of the Masses. Retrieved
from http://www.cognitiveliberty.org/5jcl/5JCL59.htm

93 *The conclusion is:* Bergland, C. (2013, November 23). One More Reason to Unplug Your
Television. *Psychology Today.* Retrieved from https://www.psychologytoday.com/blog/the-
athletes-way/201311/one-more-reason-unplug-your-television

93 *these strong connections will improve a child's physical, emotional, and social:* Bergland, C. (2013,
November 23). One More Reason to Unplug Your Television. *Psychology Today.* Retrieved
from https://www.psychologytoday.com/blog/the-athletes-way/201311/one-more-reason-
unplug-your-television

93 *According to Dr. David Walsh:* Walsh, D. A. (2012). *Smart Parenting, Smarter Kids: The One Brain
Book You Need to Help Your Child Grow Brighter, Healthier, and Happier* (p. 53). New York: Free
Press.

94 *a caregiver will speak an average of 940 words:* Hill, D. (2016, October 21). Why to Avoid TV for
Infants & Toddlers. Retrieved from https://www.healthychildren.org/English/family-
life/Media/Pages/Why-to-Avoid-TV-Before-Age-2.aspx

94 *The less a parent talks:* Hill, D. (2016, October 21). Why to Avoid TV for Infants & Toddlers.
Retrieved from https://www.healthychildren.org/English/family-life/Media/Pages/Why-
to-Avoid-TV-Before-Age-2.aspx

94 *Children's brains are designed to learn:* Hill, D. (2016, October 21). Why to Avoid TV for Infants
& Toddlers. Retrieved from https://www.healthychildren.org/English/family-

life/Media/Pages/Why-to-Avoid-TV-Before-Age-2.aspx

94   *The typical preschooler watches an average of 4 to 5 hours:* Christakis, D. *How TV Affects the Brains of Young Children* [Video file]. Retrieved February 05, 2012, from https://www.youtube.com/watch?v=v2SdEpHjrjw

94   *A 2010 study found:* Kaiser Family Foundation. (2010, January 20). Daily Media Use Among Children and Teens Up Dramatically From Five Years Ago. Retrieved from http://kff.org/disparities-policy/press-release/daily-media-use-among-children-and-teens-up-dramatically-from-five-years-ago/

95   *Psychologist and author John Rosemond:* Rosemond, J. K. (2006). *The New Six-point Plan for Raising Happy, Healthy Children.* Kansas City, MO: Andrews McMeel Pub.

95   *Some researchers believe that one reason:* Calvert, S. L., Huston, A. C., Watkins, B. A., & Wright, J. C. (1982). The Relation between Selective Attention to Television Forms and Children's Comprehension of Content. *Child Development, 53*(3), 601. doi:10.2307/1129371

96   *television is causing the shortened attention span:* National Center for Families Learning. (n.d.). Does Watching Television Affect Your Brain? Retrieved from http://wonderopolis.org/wonder/does-watching-television-affect-your-brain

96   *Because the scene or camera angle changes:* Healy, J. M. (1990). *Endangered Minds: Why Our Children Don't Think.* New York: Simon and Schuster.

96   *Because the scene or camera angle changes:* Psych Central News Editor. (2015, October 06). TV, Video Games May Increase Attention Problems. Retrieved from https://psychcentral.com/news/2010/07/05/tv-video-games-may-increase-attention-problems/15331.html

96   *Some researchers fear:* National Center for Families Learning. (n.d.). Does Watching Television Affect Your Brain? Retrieved from http://wonderopolis.org/wonder/does-watching-television-affect-your-brain

97   *There's been a 50% increase:* Kardaras, N. (2016, December 17). Kids Turn Violent as Parents Battle 'Digital Heroin' Addiction. *New York Post.* Retrieved from http://nypost.com/2016/12/17/kids-turn-violent-as-parents-battle-digital-heroin-addiction/

97   *most cases do not have any proven physical dysfunction:* Baughman, F. A., Jr. (2002). Is It a Disease or Isn't It? Retrieved from http://psychrights.org/research/Digest/ADHD/ADHDAsFraud.htm

97   *When they fail to talk through problems:* Healy, J. M. (1990). *Endangered Minds: Why Our Children Don't Think* (p. 249). New York: Simon and Schuster.

97   *One theory that links TV with ADD:* Healy, J. M. (1990). *Endangered Minds: Why Our Children Don't Think* (p. 200). New York: Simon and Schuster

97   *Researchers suggest that children, thus stimulated:* Healy, J. M. (1990). *Endangered Minds: Why Our Children Don't Think* (p. 200). New York: Simon and Schuster.

97   *neural wiring that looks like those who have ADD:* Pardley, S. (2012, December 01). *Is it Okay for My Baby or Toddler to Watch TV?* [Video file]. Retrieved from https://www.youtube.com/watch?v=mxrWVDLe3dM

98   *Family psychologist John Rosemond:* Rosemond, J. (1996, July 5). Many Professionals Give Parents Inaccurate Data on ADD. *Norman Transcript.*

98   *Neuropsychologist Dr. Jane Healy:* Healy, J. (1998, May). Understanding TV's Effects on the Developing Brain. *AAP News.*

98   *According to the Centers for Disease Control and Prevention:* Autism Society. (2014). Facts and Statistics. Retrieved from http://www.autism-society.org/what-is/facts-and-statistics/

98   *A 2015 government survey:* New Government Survey Pegs Autism Prevalence at 1 in 45. (2015, November 13). Retrieved from https://www.autismspeaks.org/science/science-news/new-government-survey-pegs-autism-prevalence-1-in-45

98   *Compare that with 1 in 2500 children:* The National Bureau of Economic Research. (2007, Winter). Does Watching Television Trigger Autism? Retrieved from http://www.nber.org/bah/winter07/w12632.htm

98   *the average age a child watched TV regularly in 1970:* Christakis, D. *How TV Affects the Brains of Young Children* [Video file]. Retrieved February 05, 2012, from https://www.youtube.com/watch?v=v2SdEpHjrjw

98   *typical preschooler is watching about 4.5 hours:* Westervelt, E. (2015, February 12). Q&A: Blocks, Play, Screen Time And The Infant Mind. Retrieved from http://www.npr.org/sections/ed/2015/02/12/385264747/q-a-blocks-play-screen-time-

and-the-infant-min

98   *Vaccinations as a cause:* Layton, J. (2006, October 18). Can TV Viewing Cause Autism? Retrieved from http://health.howstuffworks.com/mental-health/autism/tv-autism.htm

98   *According to a 2008 research study:* Layton, J. (2006, October 18). Can TV Viewing Cause Autism? Retrieved from http://health.howstuffworks.com/mental-health/autism/tv-autism.htm

98   *began to rise dramatically at the same time cable:* Layton, J. (2006, October 18). Can TV Viewing Cause Autism? Retrieved from http://health.howstuffworks.com/mental-health/autism/tv-autism.htm

98   *autism rates were higher in rainier parts:* Waldman, M. (2008). Autism Prevalence and Precipitation Rates in California, Oregon, and Washington Counties. *Archives of Pediatrics & Adolescent Medicine, 162*(11), 1026. doi:10.1001/archpedi.162.11.1026

98   *famous brain scan of the child in the Romanian orphanage:* Weir, K. (2014). The Lasting Impact of Neglect. *American Psychological Association, 45*(6). doi:10.1037/e515152014-014

98   *Researchers have found that with less talk:* Walsh, D. A. (2012). *Smart Parenting, Smarter Kids: The One Brain Book You Need to Help Your Child Grow Brighter, Healthier, and Happier* (p. 203). New York: Free Press.

99   *there's no such thing as educational TV:* Paddock, C. (2011, October 19). Babies And Toddlers Should Not Watch TV, Media Screens Say US Doctors. Retrieved from http://www.medicalnewstoday.com/

99   *literacy rate in this country was far higher:* Stedman, L. C., & Kaestle, C. F. (1987). Literacy and Reading Performance in the United States, from 1880 to the Present. *Reading Research Quarterly, 22*(1), 8. doi:10.2307/747719

99   *Studies indicate that children:* Burton, S. G., Calonico, J. M., & Mcseveney, D. R. (1979). Effects of Preschool Television Watching on First-Grade Children. *Journal of Communication, 29*(3), 164-170. doi:10.1111/j.1460-2466.1979.tb01729.x

99   *Studies indicate that children:* Shallwani, S. (2013, August 06). Effects of Television on Young Children's Learning and Development. Retrieved from https://sadafshallwani.net/2013/04/15/tv/

99   *In fact, research clearly shows:* Eisenberg, A., Murkoff, H. E., & Hathaway, S. E. (1994). *What to Expect the Toddler Years* (p. 160). New York: Workman Pub.

100 *Today, almost all American infants:* Courage, M. L., & Setliff, A. E. (2010). When Babies Watch Television: Attention-getting, Attention-holding, and the Implications for Learning from Video Material. *Developmental Review, 30*(2), 220-238. doi:10.1016/j.dr.2010.03.003

100 *If you include background television:* Kirkorian, H. L., Pempek, T. A., Murphy, L. A., Schmidt, M. E., & Anderson, D. R. (2009). The Impact of Background Television on Parent-Child Interaction. *Child Development, 80*(5), 1350-1359. doi:10.1111/j.1467-8624.2009.01337.x

100 *Pediatrician and researcher Dr. Dimitri Christakis:* Westervelt, E. (2015, February 12). Q&A: Blocks, Play, Screen Time And The Infant Mind. Retrieved from http://www.npr.org/sections/ed/2015/02/12/385264747/q-a-blocks-play-screen-time-and-the-infant-min

100 *TV viewing at age three has been linked to behavior problems:* Thompson, D. A., & Christakis, D. A. (2005). The Association Between Television Viewing and Irregular Sleep Schedules Among Children Less Than 3 Years of Age. *Pediatrics, 116*(4), 851-856. doi:10.1542/peds.2004-2788

100 *TV viewing at age three has been linked to behavior problems:* Mistry, K. B., Minkovitz, C. S., Strobino, D. M., & Borzekowski, D. L. (2007). Children's Television Exposure and Behavioral and Social Outcomes at 5.5 Years: Does Timing of Exposure Matter? *Pediatrics, 120*(4), 762-769. doi:10.1542/peds.2006-3573

101 *Watching an electronic screen one hour before bedtime:* Reverie. (2016, February 15). 3 Reasons You Shouldn't Be Watching TV Before Bed. Retrieved from http://www.reverie.com/wp/blog/3-reasons-you-shouldnt-watch-tv-before-bed#sthash.RY10vowC.dpuf

101 *This light prevents the body:* Andrew, E. (2016, August 15). Why Screen Time Before Bed Is Bad For Children. Retrieved from http://www.iflscience.com/health-and-medicine/why-screen-time-bed-bad-children/

102 *one in twelve gamers become addicted:* Walsh, D. A. (2012). *Smart Parenting, Smarter Kids: The One Brain Book You Need to Help Your Child Grow Brighter, Healthier, and Happier* (p. 215). New York: Free Press.

102 *In his book Glow Kids:* Kardaras, N. (2016). *Glow Kids: How Screen Addiction is Hijacking our Kids-*

-and How to Break the Trance. New York: St. Martin's Press.

102   *One research study done by the US Military:* Kardaras, N. (2016). Video Games Stronger Than Morphine: U.S. Military. *Psychology Today.* Retrieved from https://www.psychologytoday.com/blog/how-plato-can-save-your-life/201608/video-games-stronger-morphine-us-military

102   *the brain continues to develop until about the age of 25:* Aamodt, S., & Wang, S. (2011). *Welcome to Your Child's Brain: How the Mind Grows from Conception to College.* New York: Bloomsbury.

102   *During the teen years, the prefrontal cortex is being developed:* Walsh, D. A. (2012). *Smart Parenting, Smarter Kids: The One Brain Book You Need to Help Your Child Grow Brighter, Healthier, and Happier* (p. 215). New York: Free Press.

102   *A 2010 study:* Kaiser Family Foundation. (2010, January 20). Daily Media Use Among Children and Teens Up Dramatically From Five Years Ago. Retrieved from http://kff.org/disparities-policy/press-release/daily-media-use-among-children-and-teens-up-dramatically-from-five-years-ago/

102   *teens are spending an average of nine hours a day:* Tsukayama, H. (2015, November 3). Teens Spend Nearly Nine Hours Every Day Consuming Media. *The Washington Post.* Retrieved from https://www.washingtonpost.com/news/the-switch/wp/2015/11/03/teens-spend-nearly-nine-hours-every-day-consuming-media/?utm_term=.4c07b9ee587e

103   *problems associated with teens:* Walsh, D. A. (2012). *Smart Parenting, Smarter Kids: The One Brain Book You Need to Help Your Child Grow Brighter, Healthier, and Happier.* New York: Free Press.

103   *From The American Academy of Pediatrics:* Radesky, J., & Christakis, D. (2016). Media and Young Minds. *Pediatrics, 138*(5). Retrieved from http://pediatrics.aappublications.org/content/138/5/e20162591

104   *Author and psychologist John Rosemond:* Rosemond, J. K. (2006). *The New Xix-point Plan for Raising Happy, Healthy Children.* Kansas City, MO: Andrews McMeel Pub.

104   *Author and psychotherapist Nicholas Kardaras:* Kardaras, N. (2016, December 17). Kids Turn Violent as Parents Battle 'Digital Heroin' Addiction. *New York Post.* Retrieved from http://nypost.com/2016/12/17/kids-turn-violent-as-parents-battle-digital-heroin-addiction/

104   *While experts may disagree:* Radesky, J., & Christakis, D. (2016). Media and Young Minds. *Pediatrics, 138*(5). Retrieved from http://pediatrics.aappublications.org/content/138/5/e20162591

104   *While experts may disagree:* Boseley, S. (2012, October 08). Ban Under-Threes from Watching Television, Says Study. *The Guardian.* Retrieved from https://www.theguardian.com/society/2012/oct/09/ban-under-threes-watching-television

115   *Remember, the prefrontal cortex:* Walsh, D. A. (2012). *Smart Parenting, Smarter Kids: The One Brain Book You Need to Help Your Child Grow Brighter, Healthier, and Happier.* New York: Free Press.

ABOUT THE AUTHOR

Author and educator Katie Ely has been a school teacher for over 16 years. She also teaches parenting classes and is the creator of the *Proactive Discipline* parenting video series. In addition, she is the author of *How to Get Your Children to Clean Their Rooms Using Rubric Rules*. Katie holds a BS and a M.Ed. in Elementary Education from the University of Oklahoma and the University of Mississippi, respectively. She and her husband have two adult sons. For more practical parenting tips, visit her website The Teacher Mom at www.theteachermom.tips.

27665755R00087

Made in the USA
Lexington, KY
06 January 2019